Fathers of America's Freedom

The Story of
the Signers
of the Declaration
of Independence

by Donald E. Cooke

portrait illustrations
by Harry J. Schaare

INCORPORATED

Contents

Foreword

To many people, the signing of the Declaration of Independence recalls the painting by John Trumbull — a formal gathering of elegantly dressed gentlemen who might have had nothing more momentous on their minds than the spice trade or growing tobacco. Romanticized pictures or brief historical accounts tell us little of the human drama in the lives of the fifty-six signers.

Not only were these men putting their signatures to an explosive document that would revolutionize political thinking for generations to come but, in the view of Britain's rulers, they were literally signing their own death warrants. The broad sweep of history establishes the signing of the Declaration as an event of national and worldwide importance, but it submerges the personal feelings and, in many cases, the disastrous consequences affecting the individuals involved.

While the Revolutionary War and the power struggles of Great Britain and France raged over two continents, what was happening to the men who "pushed the button," as it were, with the point of a quill pen?

This is the story of the Declaration of Independence and, above all, of the men who drafted it and signed it. Who were they? What sort of men could dare to pledge their lives, their fortunes and their sacred honor for a new and untried concept of "government by the consent of the governed"? In the following pages are biographical sketches that may shed some light on who and what they were up to the time of signing the Declaration. Then there is the aftermath — the consequences of their endorsement.

As each one took up the pen to sign his name, even the most courageous must have wondered what lay ahead. For most of them,

trouble was inevitable. The only question was how serious the trouble would be. New York and New Jersey delegates faced almost immediate destruction of their properties by the invading British forces. Southerners may have felt temporarily more secure from the British, but were threatened by American loyalists in their own communities. New Englanders had already experienced their baptism of fire and had few illusions about the bleak future.

Nevertheless, the delegates signed the parchment bravely, and in most cases, cheerfully. Fortunately, the American army, under George Washington's remarkable leadership, managed to bring the war to a successful conclusion. Had it turned out otherwise, many of America's greatest men might have been remembered only as hot-headed rebels who wound up on the gallows, but it is doubtful that Thomas Jefferson's Declaration could have been buried with them. Within a few weeks after the adoption of the document, copies had been distributed throughout the colonies and it was being reprinted in France and circulated in the major capitals of Europe. Defeat of the Continental Army by Britain could probably have accomplished no more than to delay the inevitable revolution in political thought that had begun to grip the western world.

Again, this is the broad view of history. It tells us nothing of the anxiety, the pride, the anguish, the grief or the excitement experienced by each of the fifty-six signers after he had left his indelible mark on this great page of history. It is with such things, as well as with historical events, that this book is concerned.

Wayne, Pennsylvania
January 10, 1969   DONALD E. COOKE

PART I

Eve of Decision

The month of July in 1776 began with typical Philadelphia summer humidity. The air was hot and oppressive, the sky was overcast, and thunder rumbled west of the town. It was as though the weather shared the mood of the populace, who were gathering political forces for a different kind of storm. The roll of thunder was scarcely distinguishable from a distant beating of the drums of war.

In colonial America, war with England was already a reality. The clash with redcoats along the country lanes between Lexington and Concord had occurred more than a year earlier, on April 18, 1775, and this had been followed by the bloody Battle of Bunker Hill, or more properly, Breed's Hill, in June. An alarmed Congress was torn between those who sought a reasonable accommodation with George III and those like the fiery Sam Adams or the soberly determined Ben Frank-

lin who could see no other course but complete independence. George Washington was chosen to lead an army made up from all the colonies, and a new sovereign government of united American states began to take form.

Yet as late as January 6, 1776, the Continental Congress adopted a resolution stating that the colonies "had no design to set up as an independent nation." Many were strongly opposed to independence. Their reasons varied, but two considerations were paramount. First, the colonies were not ready for self-government, and, many believed, were incapable of defending themselves against the might of British military and naval power. Second, the colonies *were* British, and the thought of separation from the mother country was intolerable to sober men who had been brought up on traditional loyalty to the Crown.

The result was an almost unbearable political tension. Tempers flared between members of the same family. Fights over political beliefs were common in the taverns, and impassioned speeches were being delivered from pulpits and in public squares from New Hampshire down to Georgia.

Only a day or two after the January 6 resolution had been passed by Congress, a sensational pamphlet was published in Philadelphia. It appeared under the innocuous title of *Common Sense,* but it did more to stir revolutionary fervor than anything said or written up to that time. The author was Thomas Paine, an Englishman who had come to America at the urging of Benjamin Franklin. Paine was no scholar, but he had a knack of penetrating hypocrisy and exposing the plain truth. His 25,000-word book was circulated all over America and in Europe, and it sold nearly 175,000 copies in the colonies alone.

Ripping into the concept of monarchy, Paine scorned men who pretended respect for the Crown while denouncing royal edicts. "The period of debate is closed," he wrote. "Arms, as a last resort, must decide the contest."

In another passage, Paine ridiculed remote rule by Britain: "There is something very absurd in supposing a continent to be perpetually governed by an island. In no instance hath nature made the satellite larger than its primary planet: and as England and America, with respect to each other, reverse the common order of nature, it is evident that they belong to different systems."

Common Sense rocked the political thought of the civilized world, and in America it whipped up the revolutionary storm to its breaking point as the stifling heat of summer settled over the eastern seaboard.

At the center of the political thunderhead was a handsome brick building known as the State House, now famous the world over as Independence Hall. In those days it was surrounded by dwellings and stables, while in its well-trodden, grassless quadrangle stood a crude wooden platform, erected several years before for making astronomical observations. This platform was an eyesore, but within a few days it was to serve as a stage for the reading of the immortal Declaration of Independence.

Sweltering in the July heat, delegates to the Second Continental Congress strolled across the cobbles of Chestnut Street. They wore the white stockings, knee breeches, ruffled cravats and three-cornered hats of the colonial period, and their costumes were by no means tailored to cool their tempers as they sat in the stifling interior of the State House.

Shortly after Congress had assembled in the State House on July 1, news was received that a large fleet of British warships had appeared off Sandy Hook. The report heightened the tension in a room already charged with anxiety and excitement. Hot as it was, the windows were kept closed for two reasons: the first, to insure secrecy of the proceedings; the second, to keep out horseflies that swarmed in a livery stable across the street. The resulting discomfort was nearly unbearable, particularly since a good number of the biting insects found their way into the hall anyway. Frequently the oratory was punctuated by the slapping of necks and ankles as the buzzing flies drew blood.

Presiding over the assembly was John Hancock from Boston, one of the wealthiest men in the 13 colonies. Since the convening of the Second Continental Congress, Hancock had become a familiar figure on Philadelphia streets. He enjoyed taking a stroll in his expensive clothes, attended by four or five servants. Amused residents laughingly referred to him as "King Hancock," or "Hancock, the Peacock."

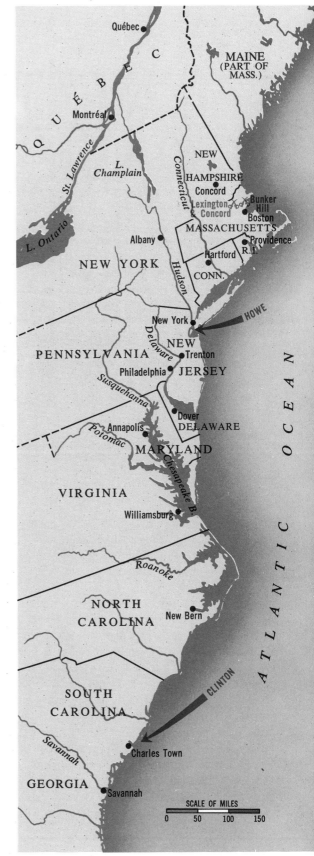

For all his finery and his royalist uncle, Hancock had no love for England's king, or for any royalty. He and Samuel Adams were the only two colonial leaders up to that time who were wanted for hanging. They were excluded from a general offer of pardon that had been extended by British General Gage in the hope of persuading the colonists to give up their "mad" quest for self rule.

The July 1 meeting opened with the reading of dispatches from General Washington, who asked for reinforcements to defend New York. As the heat of the day increased, the delegates grew restless. They listened impatiently to letters from various colonial legislatures, knowing that more important business was to be placed before them.

Assembled in the State House were between 50 and 60 men (the number fluctuated) who had been selected by various methods to represent the 13 colonies. Each colony had worked out its own plan and had made its own decision as to how many delegates it would send to the Congress. Yet each colony was permitted only one vote — always the majority opinion of that colony's delegation. If a delegation was equally split, the Clerk of Congress, Charles Thomson, recorded no vote for the colony. Delegates from Connecticut, New Jersey, New York and Maryland had been selected by their "Committees of Correspondence." These committees had been established originally to keep up secret contacts between towns and between colonies so that all sections of the country would be kept informed of developments during the growing crisis.

The colonial legislatures in Rhode Island, Massachusetts, Delaware and Pennsylvania chose their delegates to Congress, whereas in North and South Carolina, special conventions had been held for the express purpose of electing representatives. Josiah Bartlett of New Hampshire had been delegated by town

11

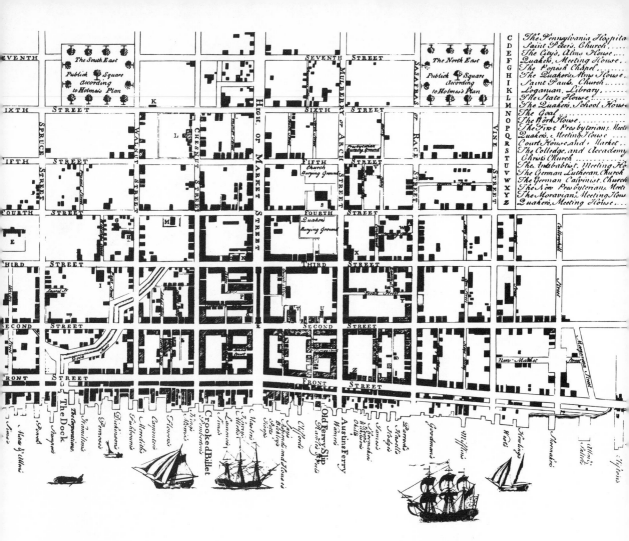

deputies. In Philadelphia, Bartlett was a busy man. As the sole representative of his colony he was expected to serve on all Congressional Committees, and this he did to the best of his ability.

After the routine reports, the Congress became alert when the chair announced that a roll call on independence would be recorded. This was to be an unofficial poll, but everyone present knew its significance. Although an effort was being made to carry a unanimous resolution, four of the colonies were still in doubt. New York representatives, who personally favored independence, were awaiting instructions. Despite the quiet persuasion of Philadelphia's senior diplomat, Benjamin Franklin, who spent most of his time trying to reassure wavering delegates, his own Pennsylvania was still opposed; so was South Carolina. The Delaware vote was evenly split — one for and one against, with a third member absent on urgent business.

While the off-the-record roll call was being taken, the sky darkened and thunder muttered close by. A motion was introduced to postpone a final vote on independence until the next day, and this was carried without opposition. Delegates scattered to their rooms or favorite ale houses as a shower spattered over the cobbled streets. The night would be tense and rainsoaked, with the great decision still to be made.

Yet in a very real sense, Congress remained in session. Much of the work — the committee meetings, the private gatherings in nearby taverns, the endless arguments — went on after the day's formal gathering adjourned.

While other delegations discussed the day's events, Thomas McKean's thoughts were concerned with his colleague, Caesar Rodney, who had returned to Delaware to help end strong loyalist activity near the town of Dover.

Realizing that the Delaware vote could be a crucial one in the effort to achieve a unanimous decision for independence, McKean had dispatched a rider with a message to Rodney, urging him to "get to Philadelphia at the earliest possible moment." As the weather was ominous, the roads poor, and the distance formidable (Dover was nearly 90 miles from Philadelphia), McKean feared that his friend would fail to arrive in time.

Caesar Rodney, the son of a prosperous planter, had been one of Congress' most active workers for independence. He was an odd-looking man — tall and lean with a face described by John Adams as "not bigger than a large apple." The left half of his countenance was concealed by a scarf which he wore to cover an advanced skin cancer. When he received McKean's message he prepared immediately for the long ride to Philadelphia. He set off in the early dusk, and rode north through torrential rain. With only a few essential stops to change horses and to take refreshment, he rode all night through downpours, wind and crashing thunder, but by dawn he was still many miles from the State House.

The other members of Congress were up early on Tuesday morning, July 2. It was customary for most of the delegates to rise at 5:00 A.M. They would breakfast, and by 6:00 were at work on committee reports or holding committee meetings prior to the general session at 9:00. On this particular morning little work was done by committees. There was only talk of the vote for independence, unofficial polling of delegates and the question of whether Delaware, South Carolina, Pennsylvania and New York could be persuaded to vote yes.

They gathered at the State House earlier than was customary. Stout old Benjamin Franklin was there, leaning on his walking stick, talking earnestly to a small group of delegates. Dr.

Franklin's expression was serious, but his eyes twinkled with irrepressible humor. It was said that he refused to write the draft of the Declaration of Independence because he would be unable to resist poking fun at the British in a way that would detract from the solemnity of the situation.

Thomas Jefferson of Virginia was there. He sat near the rear of the chamber, slouched on one hip, in a careless attitude that did not in any sense reflect his inner nervous tension. It was Jefferson who had finally accepted the task of writing the Declaration.

Samuel Adams, a Massachusetts delegate was there — the unprepossessing little man with watery eyes who had done so much to start the break with England. Adams was one of the few men of modest means in that distinguished assembly. He wore good but plain clothes that had been given to him by friends when he was elected to the Congress. Throughout his life he remained poor, devoting virtually all his time and whatever property he acquired to the cause of democracy and freedom. No other man contributed more to the Revolution. His fiery speeches had roused people to the point where they attacked British troops in Boston on March 5, 1770, resulting in the Boston Massacre. It was Adams who organized and inspired the "Boston Tea Party" in 1773 to protest the arrival of a shipment of British tea. His activities with the Sons of Liberty and the Committee of Correspondence had made Boston the cockpit of rebellion.

Most of the men who would sign the Declaration of Independence — and some who did not sign — were at the State House that morning of July 2nd. The weather continued close and overcast. The streets remained wet from the night's showers. Missing still was Caesar Rodney as the hour of 9:00 approached and the rain began to fall again.

Notable for their absence were Pennsyl-

13

vania delegates Robert Morris and John Dickinson. Since it was well known that they had been opposed to a declaration of independence, their failure to appear at this crucial moment was significant — an apparent gesture of unspoken approval. Delaware's Thomas McKean stood at the back of the hall, watching the door anxiously. Word was being passed among the delegates that Pennsylvania, New York and South Carolina had finally been won over. Now the Delaware vote was vitally important.

John Hancock, fashionably dressed as always, looked over the assemblage and prepared to open the meeting. At that instant, the clatter of hoofs sounded on the cobbles outside; a moment later a gaunt, bedraggled figure strode into the large room. It was Caesar Rodney. He still wore his mud-caked riding boots and spurs, and he was soaked to the skin. As he took his seat with McKean, the meeting was called to order. The clerk, Mr. Thomson read a resolution, the words of which were already familiar to the delegates. These courageous proposals had been penned and introduced to Congress on June 7 by Richard Henry Lee of Virginia:

"Resolved that these United Colonies are, and of right ought to be, free and independent States, that they are absolved from all allegiance to the British Crown and that all political connection between them and the State of Great Britain is, and ought to be, totally dissolved.

"That it is expedient forthwith to take the most effectual measures for forming foreign alliances.

"That a plan of confederation be prepared and transmitted to the colonies for their consideration and approbation."

Chairman of the Committee of the Whole to consider the resolution on independence was Benjamin Harrison, a large, jovial man who had skillfully chaired and moderated every meeting and debate on the measure.

Now the vote was being recorded. As was customary they began with the northernmost colonies and proceeded from New Hampshire southward to Georgia. The New England vote was solidly for independence. The New York delegates abstained once again, though all were sure by this time that their instructions, when they should arrive, would be to vote "aye." New Jersey voted affirmatively and, in the absence of Morris and Dickinson, Pennsylvania followed suit. Next Thomson asked for Delaware's vote. In behalf of that colony, Caesar Rodney rose to his feet and spoke in a weary but clear voice, "As I believe the voice of my constituents and of all sensible and honest men is in favor of independence and my own judgment concurs with them, I vote for Independence."

So it went, straight through the roll. The vote was, indeed, unanimous — 12 colonies in favor of separation from England, and one abstention. Charles Thomson made the appropriate entry in his journal, and the thing was done.

But the consequences could only be guessed. Every man in the room knew that the decreed British penalty for their action was death by hanging. Most of them must have been thinking of their homes and families and what might now occur in the various colonies during their absence. For the moment, however, little time was permitted to ponder the gloomy prospects. Thomas Jefferson's paper was now to be considered, and there was divergence of opinion as to the document's wording. As the day wore on and it became clear that the delegates were not prepared to approve the Declaration as it stood, it was decided to adjourn and to devote the next day to debating Jefferson's draft.

The great decision had been made. Now would come the work, the bloodshed and the heartache of implementing it.

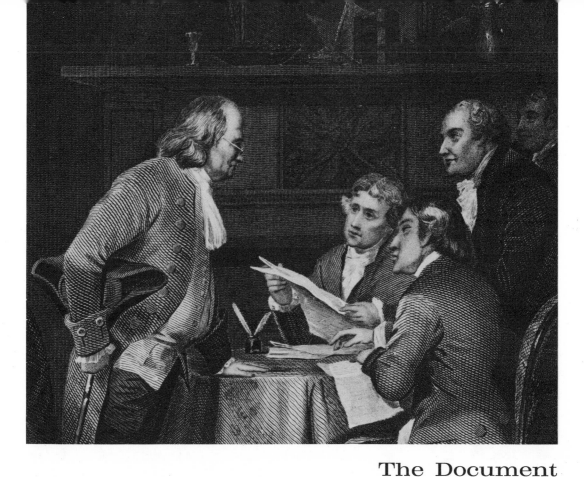

The Document

The man who had been chosen to put America's quest for independence into words was Thomas Jefferson, the Virginia delegate who had been elected to the drafting committee. This committee, established three days after the introduction of Richard Henry Lee's resolutions, consisted of John Adams of Massachusetts, Benjamin Franklin of Pennsylvania, Roger Sherman of Connecticut, Robert R. Livingston of New York and the Virginian, Thomas Jefferson.

No committee of the Second Continental Congress bore a greater responsibility. On the statement they were expected to write rested the future of mankind, and the five committee members were well aware of it. At the outset, the committee debated among themselves as to who was best suited to do the actual writing. Thomas Jefferson originally urged John Adams to accept the task. When Adams refused, he pointed out that Jefferson himself was the logical author. "Reason first," he said, "you are a Virginian, and Virginia ought to appear at the head of this business.

Reason second, I am obnoxious, suspected and unpopular; You are very much otherwise. Reason third, you can write ten times better than I can."

"Well," replied Jefferson, "if you are decided, I will do as well as I can."*

The insistence of John Adams that a Virginian do the writing was soundly based. Delegates from all the colonies were familiar with Virginia's historic roll in the rebellion. In March 1775, a convention had been held at St. John's Church, Richmond, Virginia, and there George Washington, Thomas Jefferson, Richard Henry Lee and many other prominent Virginians heard Patrick Henry speak in a voice that would reverberate through the endless corridors of human history, "I know not how others may feel, but as for me, give me liberty or give me death!"

While others might argue that the greatest activists of the revolution were the two Massachusetts cousins, John and Samuel Adams,

* Adams to Timothy Pickering — The Works of John Adams

15

Left
Portable writing desk used by Jefferson
in writing the Declaration

Right
A portion of Jefferson's "rough draft"

the fact remained that much of the eloquence flowed from Virginia's scholars.

From his days as a young lawyer, Jefferson's views on freedom and human rights had been unorthodox for that time and place. As early as 1770 he had spoken out against slavery. In a court case involving the enslavement of a grandchild of a white woman and a Negro man, he argued, "Under the law of nature, all men are born free, everyone comes into the world with a right to his own person, which includes the liberty of moving and using it at his own will."

The court ruled his argument invalid.

However, other Virginians agreed with his ideas and supported him in the Virginia House of Burgesses. Despite his views on slavery he was considered to be less of an extremist than many of the Virginians of his generation.

During Jefferson's term with the Second Continental Congress he rented two second floor rooms in the house of Frederic Graff, a bricklayer by trade. The red brick house was on the southwest corner of Seventh and Market Streets in Philadelphia, a location considered to be "on the edge of town," and it was there that the Declaration of Independence was written. Jefferson worked on a portable writing desk which he held on his knees. He had invented and designed the desk himself and had ordered it made by a former landlord named Benjamin Randolph.

For several days he scratched away with his quill, crossing out phrases, inserting others, rewriting and refining. As he had also authored the recently adopted Virginia Bill of Rights, it was natural that he should paraphrase its opening words, "...all men are born equally free and independent and have

certain inherent rights — among which are enjoyment of life, liberty and pursuing and obtaining happiness and safety."

Essentially, this was the thought expressed in the final Declaration, but the sentence was improved both in its literary style and in its directness, as Jefferson realized that while pursuing happiness was a basic right, obtaining it was not:

"We hold these truths to be self-evident: That all men are created equal; that they are endowed by their creator with certain inalienable rights; that among these are life, liberty and the pursuit of happiness."

Jefferson's first rough draft was generally approved by John Adams, who nevertheless felt that some passages showed the harshness — and consequent weakness — of anger. Adams questioned the anti-slavery passages which occupied a prominent place in the draft. He argued that direct reference to the evils of slavery might so antagonize the southern delegations that the entire cause might founder.

The early version included the phrase, "The King of Great Britain kept open a market where men were bought and sold, and prostituted his negative by suppressing Virginia's legislative attempts to restrain this execrable commerce." Jefferson insisted on keeping this sentence in the draft, but as Adams predicted, Congress struck it out.

Benjamin Franklin was less critical of the draft, though he did do some minor editing of the wording.

The other committee members, Roger Sherman and Robert Livingston, apparently made their contributions through discussion of specific points in the document. Roger Sherman, considered to be one of the most level-headed

When in the course of human events it becomes necessary for one people to dissolve the political bands which have connected them with another, and to assume among the powers of the earth the separate and equal station to which the laws of nature & of nature's god entitle them, a decent respect to the opinions of mankind requires that they should declare the causes which impel them to the separation.

We hold these truths to be self-evident; that all men are created equal, that they are endowed by their creator with

members of the Congress, helped to temper Jefferson's fiery prose. He was a quiet, sober Puritan who had begun his career as a cobbler and had taught himself law by propping books before him on his cobbler's bench. John Adams said of him, ". . . he was one of the most sensible men in the world. The clearest head and the steadiest heart."

Although Robert Livingston served on the drafting committee, he never signed the document he had helped to create, as he was no longer in the Congress at the time of the actual signing, and in point of fact he was never enthusiastic about a full break with Great Britain. A prosperous New York lawyer and a landowner, his views were more conservative than those of most of his colleagues. He was elected to the committee at the urging of Sam Adams who felt it would help win votes of other conservative delegates to have a restraining hand involved in the drafting.

Regardless of any help or advice provided by the other committee members, Thomas Jefferson was the real author of the Declaration. After discussing the form of the composition with the committee, he agreed that not only must he make clear to Britain the reasons for separation, but he must justify the rebellious action with all the nations of the world. Further, the Declaration must serve as a catalyst to hold the separate colonies together and to help weld a solid union. It was an awesome assignment.

He titled his first draft, *A Declaration by the Representatives of the United States of America, in General Congress Assembled*. His beginning in the original read as follows:

"When in the course of Human events it becomes necessary for a people to advance from that subordination in which they have hitherto remained, & to assume among the powers of the earth the equal & independent station to which the laws of nature & nature's god entitled them, a decent respect to the opinions of mankind requires that they should declare the causes which impel them to the change."

Jefferson's quill pen rushed on, and the words began to flow with greater eloquence as he outlined the "truths" which he held to be "sacred & undeniable." It was here that he drew upon his earlier composition of the Virginia Bill of Rights, stating the fundamental concept of Man's natural freedom that would stand as the cornerstone for the entire human rights structure. Much of his philosophy could be traced to the writings of another Virginian, George Mason, and to John Locke's well-known *Treatises of Civil Government*. But to those earlier writings, Jefferson added a clarity and brilliant logic that was purely his own. Up to that time, nearly all discussions of human rights had considered ownership of property to be the justification for most other rights. While Jefferson agreed that every man had a right to own property, and that it was a function of government to protect that property, he recognized that the *lack* of possessions in no way diminished a man's right to take part in government or his right to life, liberty and the pursuit of happiness.

One of the momentous phrases in Jefferson's declaration was that "governments are instituted among men, deriving their just powers *from the consent of the governed*." Here was the foundation of the entire revolutionary movement — a concept that would shake the world and bring about the downfall of most of Europe's monarchies. Yet he introduced the idea so casually and followed it with such reasonable statements about traditional, "long established governments," that the conservative delegates in Congress could find no fault.

"Prudence," he said, "will dictate that governments long established should *not* be changed for light & transient causes; and accordingly all experience hath shewn that mankind are more disposed to suffer while evils are sufferable, than to right themselves by abolishing the forms to which they are accustomed."

Still, he argued, the list of grievances against the British Crown was so long and so heavy with injustice that America must provide new guards for its future security.

The struggle to present the colonial case simply, and powerfully, and to include all the desired ingredients must have brought Jefferson near to a state of mental exhaustion by the time his draft was completed. When the day arrived for Congress to discuss his work— to criticize it and debate the value of each sentence — he must have suffered agony. Already he and the committee members had made more than thirty changes in the first draft. Probably the committee discussions had been heated at times. The paper, riddled with insertions and deletions was finally recopied by Jefferson, and it was this second draft that was now in the ungentle hands of Congress. It had been awaiting final approval since it was handed over on June 28.

When the delegates assembled on Wednesday, July 3, the rains of the past two days had ended. It was a fine, clear day — the kind that stirs the blood. While Jefferson nervously took a seat at the back of the hall, his portable writing desk on his lap, the representatives plunged into their task with enthusiasm. The first two paragraphs of the Declaration were read and passed almost as Jefferson had written them. The few minor alterations in the

introduction included changing "inherent & inalienable rights" to "certain unalienable rights." (Most experts believe that the *un* was a printer's error and not an editorial change requested by Congress.)

A heated discussion developed, as expected, over Jefferson's references to slavery and the African slave trade. Finally northern and liberal southern delegates acceded to the demands of southern slaveholders by deleting the slave trade charge. Jefferson himself made notes of the proposed changes, seethed inwardly, but said nothing. His chief defender was the dauntless John Adams whom Jefferson later described as "our colossus on the floor . . . not graceful nor eloquent, nor remarkably fluent, but he came out . . . with a power of thought and expression, that moved us from our seats."

John Dickinson of New Jersey still attempted to dissuade Congress from making any formal declaration of independence. In the earlier debate over independence, on July 1 he had asked, "What advantages are to be obtained from such a declaration?" Foreign powers would want to see deeds, not words, he argued; further, "this Declaration may weaken the Union, when the people find themselves engaged in a cause rendered more cruel by such a Declaration without prospect of an end to their Calamities, by a continuation of the war."

The conclusion of Dickinson's eloquent speech had been greeted by a chilling silence. Clearly the delegates who had begun the discussion with patriotic zeal were now moved to doubts and second thoughts. It was at this point that Edward Rutledge had come over to where John Adams was seated and begged him to speak in defense of the declaration. Adams did so, reluctantly, for he had used the arguments so many times he feared they had gone stale. Yet his spontaneous speech which was only partially recorded, was probably one

of the best — certainly one of the most important — of his political career.

"This is the first time of my life," he told the delegates, "that I have ever wished for the talents and eloquence of the ancient orators of Greece and Rome, for I am sure that none of them ever had before him a question of more importance to his country and to the world."

Adams then proceeded to reaffirm the faith of the great majority of delegates in the fateful step they were about to take. Yet he made no attempt to gloss over the dangers confronting them: "If you imagine that I expect this declaration will ward off calamities from this country, you are much mistaken. A bloody conflict we are destined to endure."

The debate on July 3 lasted several hours, and the session adjourned without final approval of the document. On July 4, the merciless editing of Jefferson's writing continued, and it was in the latter portion of the document, the list of grievances against King George and the British government, that most of the changes were made. Out of the original 1817 words, 480 were cut while Jefferson suffered in silence.

The revision was completed some time in the evening of July 4, 1776, and the adoption of the Declaration of Independence "by the representatives of the United States of America in General Congress Assembled" was duly recorded as of that date. In spite of Jefferson's natural resentment of the extensive cuts in his work, the manuscript was, on the whole, improved by the work of those fifty-odd critics. The final result left only the essential points and a direct, uncluttered statement of principles. Possibly by the time the final vote of approval was taken, the delegates were too weary to argue further, or they might have overdone a good job.

The only person to sign the document that day was the president of Congress, John Hancock, whose signature was attested by Secretary Charles Thomson. In the final action of the day Congress ordered that copies of the Declaration were to be printed that night, and that independence should be declared throughout the United *States*. The word "colony" no longer appeared in the records.

As Congress adjourned that evening, the great bell in the State House tower was rung. An expectant crowd that had been gathering in the square all afternoon cheered wildly. Suddenly the quiet town was aroused. Cannon boomed; church bells clashed and clanged from Front Street on the Delaware, to the Schuylkill River, two miles to the west, and riders were dispatched to carry the momentous story to other towns and colonies.

That night, printer John Dunlap ran off a number of large 15- by 18-inch copies of the Declaration. These were posted in prominent places and were read in village squares, markets, from the pulpits of churches and in army camps. General Washington directed that the Declaration was to be read to each brigade of the army on the evening of July 9.

For several days, spontaneous parades and celebrations were held in communities all over the country. Occasionally violence erupted. In Bowling Green, New York, a huge equestrian statue of George III was roped and pulled to the ground. Gleefully, the crowd hacked it to pieces and the chunks of royal metal were carted to the home of General Oliver Wolcott in Connecticut, where his wife and other ladies of the town melted them and cast the metal into more than 42,000 bullets.

The day for a formal signing of the Declaration was set by Congress, and in preparation for this, the document was ordered engrossed on parchment by a skilled calligrapher named Timothy Matlack.

In the meantime, there was a public reading of the Declaration at the State House yard in Philadelphia. Colonel John Nixon, standing on the wooden observation platform and flanked by several important members of Congress, read the document to a large crowd of citizens on July 8. Not until July 9 did the New York State Convention vote to permit their delegates to vote approval of the Declaration. They formally cast their "aye" vote on July 15, and on that day the title of the document was changed to "The Unanimous Declaration of the Thirteen United States of America."

After the handsomely engrossed parchment copy was completed, on August 2, Congress gathered in the State House for the signing. Whether or not it had been intended from the beginning that all delegates should sign the Declaration is not clear, but at some point it was agreed that the general signing should be made for the protection of all. There was, perhaps, some safety in numbers, although none doubted that each signer was "putting his head in the noose" by his action.

Delegate William Ellery of Rhode Island took up a position where he could see each member as he wrote his name. "I was determined," he wrote afterward, "to see how they all looked as they signed what might be their death warrants. I placed myself beside the secretary, Charles Thomson, and eyed each closely as he affixed his name to the document. Undaunted resolution was displayed on every countenance."

John Hancock, who signed first, penned his large, flourishing signature which he had developed in penmanship class at a Boston Latin School. "John Bull can read my name without spectacles," he said, "and may now double his reward of £500 for my head."

The other delegates signed in the usual geographical order of states from north to south, so that George Walton of Georgia was the last to enter his name that day. Between July 4 when the final version of the Declaration was approved and the formal signing on August 2, there had been a number of changes in Congress. Some delegates had left and been replaced. Others who had been absent for the vote were present at the signing. One of these was Robert Morris. New members on August 2 included Benjamin Rush, George Clymer, James Smith, George Taylor and George Ross of Pennsylvania. Virginia's Richard Henry Lee, who had initiated the original resolution for independence, was absent on the day of the vote as well as on August 2, but he returned to sign at an unknown later date. Samuel Chase of Maryland also signed later. One of the delegates who voted against independence, but who signed the document nevertheless, was George Read of Delaware. Probably the last signature to be added in 1776 was that of Matthew Thornton, Irish-born New Hampshire representative who was not elected to the Congress until the twelfth of September and was not seated until November. He signed the Declaration a few days after his arrival in Philadelphia.

When Congress moved from Philadelphia to Baltimore in December, 1776, all official papers were removed from the State House, including the Declaration. In Baltimore, a new printing was made, less hastily and with fewer errors. All names of the signers were included on this printing, with the single exception of Thomas McKean of Delaware. Evidently he signed last of all, some time in 1777.

The 56 courageous men who had put their names to the historic document had taken perilous steps in a direction from which there was no turning. Yet they wrote their names without the slightest hesitation. Only one signer's hand shook so that the signature was scarcely more than an irregular scratch. This was Stephen Hopkins of Rhode Island, the second oldest delegate who suffered from severe palsy. As he handed over the quill to Ellery, he remarked, "My hand trembles, but my heart does not!"

The engrossed and signed manuscript
of the Declaration of Independence

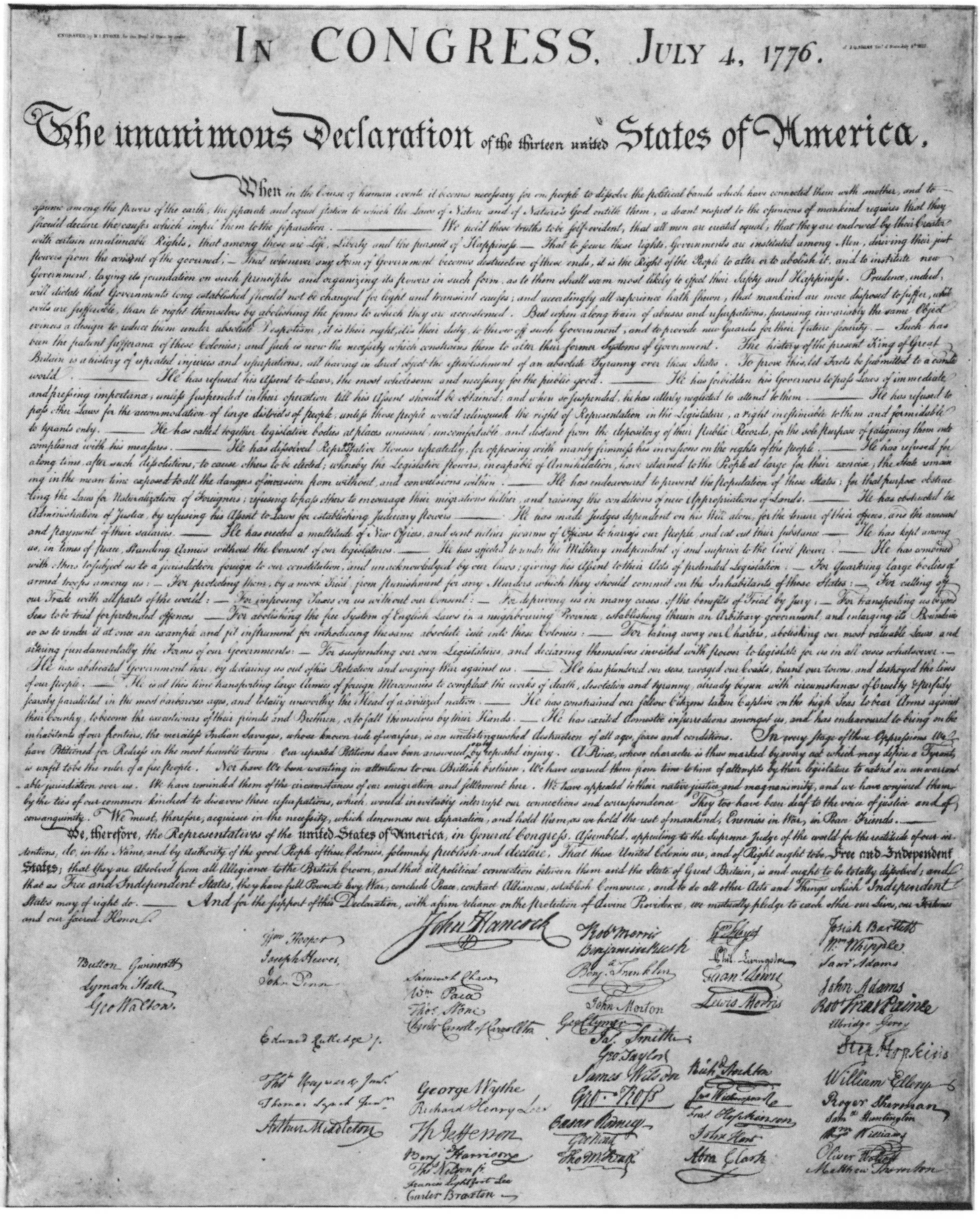
IN CONGRESS, JULY 4, 1776.

The unanimous Declaration of the thirteen united States of America,

When in the Course of human events, it becomes necessary for one people to dissolve the political bands which have connected them with another, and to assume among the powers of the earth, the separate and equal station to which the Laws of Nature and of Nature's God entitle them, a decent respect to the opinions of mankind requires that they should declare the causes which impel them to the separation. — We hold these truths to be self-evident, that all men are created equal, that they are endowed by their Creator with certain unalienable Rights, that among these are Life, Liberty and the pursuit of Happiness. — That to secure these rights, Governments are instituted among Men, deriving their just powers from the consent of the governed, — That whenever any Form of Government becomes destructive of these ends, it is the Right of the People to alter or to abolish it, and to institute new Government, laying its foundation on such principles and organizing its powers in such form, as to them shall seem most likely to effect their Safety and Happiness. Prudence, indeed, will dictate that Governments long established should not be changed for light and transient causes; and accordingly all experience hath shewn, that mankind are more disposed to suffer, while evils are sufferable, than to right themselves by abolishing the forms to which they are accustomed. But when a long train of abuses and usurpations, pursuing invariably the same Object evinces a design to reduce them under absolute Despotism, it is their right, it is their duty, to throw off such Government, and to provide new Guards for their future security. — Such has been the patient sufferance of these Colonies; and such is now the necessity which constrains them to alter their former Systems of Government. The history of the present King of Great Britain is a history of repeated injuries and usurpations, all having in direct object the establishment of an absolute Tyranny over these States. To prove this, let Facts be submitted to a candid world. — He has refused his Assent to Laws, the most wholesome and necessary for the public good. — He has forbidden his Governors to pass Laws of immediate and pressing importance, unless suspended in their operation till his Assent should be obtained; and when so suspended, he has utterly neglected to attend to them. — He has refused to pass other Laws for the accommodation of large districts of people, unless those people would relinquish the right of Representation in the Legislature, a right inestimable to them and formidable to tyrants only. — He has called together legislative bodies at places unusual, uncomfortable, and distant from the depository of their public Records, for the sole purpose of fatiguing them into compliance with his measures. — He has dissolved Representative Houses repeatedly, for opposing with manly firmness his invasions on the rights of the people. — He has refused for a long time, after such dissolutions, to cause others to be elected; whereby the Legislative powers, incapable of Annihilation, have returned to the People at large for their exercise; the State remaining in the mean time exposed to all the dangers of invasion from without, and convulsions within. — He has endeavoured to prevent the population of these States; for that purpose obstructing the Laws for Naturalization of Foreigners; refusing to pass others to encourage their migrations hither, and raising the conditions of new Appropriations of Lands. — He has obstructed the Administration of Justice, by refusing his Assent to Laws for establishing Judiciary powers. — He has made Judges dependent on his Will alone, for the tenure of their offices, and the amount and payment of their salaries. — He has erected a multitude of New Offices, and sent hither swarms of Officers to harrass our people, and eat out their substance. — He has kept among us, in times of peace, Standing Armies without the Consent of our legislatures. — He has affected to render the Military independent of and superior to the Civil power. — He has combined with others to subject us to a jurisdiction foreign to our constitution, and unacknowledged by our laws; giving his Assent to their Acts of pretended Legislation: — For Quartering large bodies of armed troops among us: — For protecting them, by a mock Trial, from punishment for any Murders which they should commit on the Inhabitants of these States: — For cutting off our Trade with all parts of the world: — For imposing Taxes on us without our Consent: — For depriving us in many cases, of the benefits of Trial by Jury: — For transporting us beyond Seas to be tried for pretended offences — For abolishing the free System of English Laws in a neighbouring Province, establishing therein an Arbitrary government, and enlarging its Boundaries so as to render it at once an example and fit instrument for introducing the same absolute rule into these Colonies: — For taking away our Charters, abolishing our most valuable Laws, and altering fundamentally the Forms of our Governments: — For suspending our own Legislatures, and declaring themselves invested with power to legislate for us in all cases whatsoever. — He has abdicated Government here, by declaring us out of his Protection and waging War against us. — He has plundered our seas, ravaged our Coasts, burnt our towns, and destroyed the lives of our people. — He is at this time transporting large Armies of foreign Mercenaries to compleat the works of death, desolation and tyranny, already begun with circumstances of Cruelty & perfidy scarcely paralleled in the most barbarous ages, and totally unworthy the Head of a civilized nation. — He has constrained our fellow Citizens taken Captive on the high Seas to bear Arms against their Country, to become the executioners of their friends and Brethren, or to fall themselves by their Hands. — He has excited domestic insurrections amongst us, and has endeavoured to bring on the inhabitants of our frontiers, the merciless Indian Savages, whose known rule of warfare, is an undistinguished destruction of all ages, sexes and conditions. In every stage of these Oppressions We have Petitioned for Redress in the most humble terms: Our repeated Petitions have been answered only by repeated injury. A Prince, whose character is thus marked by every act which may define a Tyrant, is unfit to be the ruler of a free people. Nor have We been wanting in attentions to our Brittish brethren. We have warned them from time to time of attempts by their legislature to extend an unwarrantable jurisdiction over us. We have reminded them of the circumstances of our emigration and settlement here. We have appealed to their native justice and magnanimity, and we have conjured them by the ties of our common kindred to disavow these usurpations, which, would inevitably interrupt our connections and correspondence. They too have been deaf to the voice of justice and of consanguinity. We must, therefore, acquiesce in the necessity, which denounces our Separation, and hold them, as we hold the rest of mankind, Enemies in War, in Peace Friends.

We, therefore, the Representatives of the united States of America, in General Congress, Assembled, appealing to the Supreme Judge of the world for the rectitude of our intentions, do, in the Name, and by Authority of the good People of these Colonies, solemnly publish and declare, That these United Colonies are, and of Right ought to be Free and Independent States; that they are Absolved from all Allegiance to the British Crown, and that all political connection between them and the State of Great Britain, is and ought to be totally dissolved; and that as Free and Independent States, they have full Power to levy War, conclude Peace, contract Alliances, establish Commerce, and to do all other Acts and Things which Independent States may of right do. — And for the support of this Declaration, with a firm reliance on the protection of divine Providence, we mutually pledge to each other our Lives, our Fortunes and our sacred Honor.

John Hancock

Button Gwinnett
Lyman Hall
Geo Walton.

Wm Hooper
Joseph Hewes,
John Penn

Edward Rutledge 1.
Thos Heyward Junr.
Thomas Lynch Junr.
Arthur Middleton

Samuel Chase
Wm. Paca
Thos. Stone
Charles Carroll of Carrollton

George Wythe
Richard Henry Lee
Th Jefferson
Benja Harrison
Thos Nelson jr.
Francis Lightfoot Lee
Carter Braxton

Robt Morris
Benjamin Rush
Benja. Franklin
John Morton
Geo Clymer
Jas. Smith.
Geo. Taylor
James Wilson
Geo. Ross
Caesar Rodney
Geo Read
Tho M:Kean

Wm Floyd
Phil. Livingston
Frans. Lewis
Lewis Morris
Richd. Stockton
Jno Witherspoon
Fras. Hopkinson
John Hart
Abra Clark

Josiah Bartlett
Wm. Whipple
Saml Adams
John Adams
Robt Treat Paine
Elbridge Gerry
Step. Hopkins
William Ellery
Roger Sherman
Sam.el Huntington
Wm. Williams
Oliver Wolcott
Matthew Thornton

PART II

The Signers

From his vantage point close to the table where the parchment rested, William Ellery of Rhode Island observed the faces of fifty men as they affixed their signatures to the document. These were, for the most part, sober members of a well-to-do society—landowners, lawyers, merchants, doctors and educators. They came to the table in groups, by delegations. Each man dipped a large quill pen into a pot of ink, wrote his name, and moved toward the back of the hall to converse in low tones with his compatriots. The act of signing was a simple one, but its implications and long-range effects were vast.

Although the weather had moderated, the interior of the hall still retained the heat of the past few days, yet none of the delegates seemed to notice. Their mission absorbed their attention. Ellery knew them all, some intimately, others by reputation, and he could scarcely be blamed for taking pride in being a member of such a group. Their ages ranged

Congress voting Independence,
July 4, 1776

was already in progress—a war that so far was not going well for Washington's ill-equipped army. Undoubtedly many of the signers glanced at the final sentence of the Declaration, just above their signatures, as they picked up the quill: "And for the support of this declaration, with a firm reliance on the protection of Divine Providence, we mutually pledge to each other our lives, our fortunes, and our sacred honor."

This was no mere rhetoric—no high-sounding phrase for effect. The pledge meant exactly what it said, and many of the men in that room were destined to sacrifice their lives and their fortunes to the cause they had endorsed.

What did William Ellery see in the faces of the delegates? What sort of men were they who dared to risk everything they had for a new and revolutionary idea? Here were no hot-blooded radicals from the universities, dreamers whose heads were filled with theoretical nonsense, no poverty-stricken outcasts with nothing to lose. From a standpoint of material well-being, most of them could gain nothing; many could—and would—lose great wealth. Why, then, did they sign the Declaration so eagerly?

The answer was in the character of the men and of the times. Believing absolutely in the rightness of the step they took, it was a matter of sacred honor to uphold it, come what may. They understood, as few men do, that wealth of the mind and of the spirit is more to be cherished than all the material possessions of a Midas. What brought them to the State House, what led each man to the table and to the signing of the Declaration varied with individual training and circumstances. They had debated the issue long and thoroughly; there had been disagreements. But having finally agreed on independence they were now determined as one to fight to the death for it.

from 26 (Edward Rutledge of South Carolina) to 70 (Benjamin Franklin of Pennsylvania). Though they were men of divergent background and temperament their common purpose in this gathering welded them into a mighty atom of political force. As Benjamin Franklin was reported to have said to them, "We must all hang together, or most assuredly we shall all hang separately."

The atmosphere in the State House that day was apparently calm enough, but a war

William Ellery watched the first signer with particular interest, for here was not only the President of the Second Continental Congress and as such, a "ringleader" in British eyes, but he was one of the wealthiest and most influential men in America. His birthplace was Braintree (renamed Quincy), Massachusetts. His father, a Puritan clergyman, died when John Hancock was seven. He was afterwards supported by Thomas Hancock, an uncle, who was considered to be the most prosperous merchant in Boston. From the uncle, John inherited his luxurious home on Beacon Hill along with the uncle's shipping firm and a fortune in money and properties.

At the age of seventeen Hancock had graduated from Harvard College. Within ten years he was one of New England's foremost merchants, a leader in his community, and even wealthier than his uncle had been before him. British regulations restricting colonial trade were of direct concern to John Hancock's interests. He therefore vigorously opposed the 1765 Stamp Act, and one of his sloops, the *Liberty,* was seized by British authorities for his refusal to pay duties. His courageous stand made him a popular figure throughout New England. This remarkable man of fortune did not allow his love of luxuried living to stifle his anger over England's unjust behavior. He made it clear that nothing would deter him in the fight to rid Boston of British troops when he remarked, "Burn Boston and make John Hancock a beggar, if the public good requires it."

He was involved in politics as early as 1769, when he was elected to the Massachusetts legislature, known at that time as the "General Court." In 1770 he was in the forefront of a movement demanding withdrawal of British troops from Boston. After British General Gage issued an order forbidding the establishment of a provincial government, Hancock was elected president of the Massachusetts congress which first met in Concord.

It was on April 18, 1775, about six months after he had become president of the provincial congress, when Hancock and Samuel Adams were aroused in the night by Paul Revere, who had made a wild ride from Boston to warn them that the British were on their way to seize them. Hancock had been enjoying a pleasant dinner with his fiancee, Dorothy Quincy, at the parsonage of Rev. Jonas Clarke when the warning was brought by Revere. As Adams and Hancock made their departure, Revere rode on, urging citizens to arm themselves and to prepare to fight the British. The two patriot leaders had barely escaped when the first shots of the Revolution echoed along the country lanes near Lexington.

As an elected Massachusetts delegate to the Second Continental Congress, John Hancock took his seat in Philadelphia early in May 1775. Within a few days, the Congressional president, Peyton Randolph, resigned and Hancock was unanimously chosen to replace him. As efforts were made to organize a Continental Army, Hancock confidently expected to be made the commander-in-chief, but he was disappointed to learn that other delegates had selected George Washington of Virginia. The choice was partly political, since many northern delegates hoped, by this means, to assure the South's support in the coming struggle. Later, the egotistical Hancock showed his resentment by discussing military plans with subordinate generals without consulting Washington.

With the signing of the Declaration of Independence, John Hancock's name became immortal. Legend has it that John Hancock said that he had written his signature large enough for John Bull to read it without his glasses. His name stands out boldly so that even today it is synonymous with the word "signature."

NEW
HAMPSHIRE
Concord
Portsmouth
Kingston

Josiah Bartlett

Wm Whipple

Matthew Thornton

The New Hampshire delegation, composed of two members, followed John Hancock to the table. Second to sign the Declaration was Josiah Bartlett, a physician who had gained a wide reputation through effective use of a Peruvian bark called cinchona. His discovery of the medicinal qualities of this bark occurred years before the more concentrated quinine was extracted from it.

Bartlett was born November 21, 1729, in Amesbury, Massachusetts, and from his earliest years he had been determined to become a doctor. After he had learned medicine under the tutelage of another physician he began practice in Kingston, New Hampshire, at the age of twenty-one. Always a leader in his community, he was elected to the New Hampshire Assembly in 1765, and was appointed a colonel of militia by the royal governor of the colony. Although he was highly favored by the British authorities, Bartlett immediately joined with the colonists as the struggle for independence developed. His support of the patriot cause led to his dismissal as a justice of the peace and, presumably, to the burning of his house by a British agent in 1774. He worked on the New Hampshire Committee of Correspondence until his election to the Second Continental Congress. As Josiah Bartlett took up the quill to put his name to the document, William Ellery saw a rugged-looking man in his forties. Bartlett was tall, his curly hair had a reddish tint, and he moved with determination and vigor. When the vote for independence had been tallied, he had "made the rafters echo

with his approval," according to fellow delegates. Now he had the privilege of being the first of the regular delegates to sign the Declaration.

William Whipple was the second New Hampshire delegate to take up the quill. A well-to-do merchant, Whipple had at one time been the captain of a ship plying the West Indies trade. At twenty-nine, he took his savings, retired from the sea and entered into a successful mercantile partnership with his brother, Joseph. In 1775, he began to take part in meetings of New Hampshire patriots and was elected to the local Committee of Safety. This led to his selection by the legislature to serve as a representative of New Hampshire in the Second Continental Congress. By this time he had relinquished his

JOSIAH BARTLETT

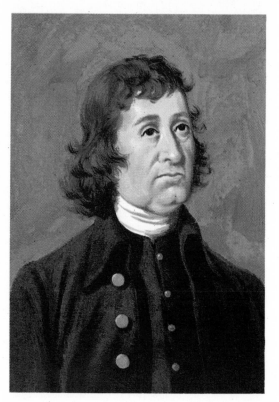

part in the business in order to devote his full time to the struggle for independence.

New Hampshire had yet another signer, Matthew Thornton, also a physician. He was not present at the formal signing, as he was elected to the Continental Congress in September, and did not take his seat until November 1776. Thus although he had no opportunity to vote for independence, he asked permission to sign the Declaration and added his name to the document on November 19. He was sixty-two at the time. Thornton had served as a military surgeon in the British colonial army thirty years earlier, and had accompanied some five hundred New Hampshire militia on an expedition that attacked the French in Nova Scotia. A native of Ireland, he had come to America with his parents at the age of four. He was a spirited story teller who loved to regale lis-

teners with humorous anecdotes and fables. He had a knack for capturing and holding the attention of those around him. After his early schooling in Massachusetts, Thornton had studied medicine under an established physician by the name of Grout, and had begun his own practice when he was twenty-six. A few years before the Revolution he became a member of the New Hampshire legislature. As trouble with England developed, he threw all his energy behind the patriot cause, was elected president of New Hampshire's provincial legislature, and as chairman of the regional Committee of Safety, was active in collecting arms and recruiting militia for the colony. After serving briefly as speaker of the newly organized New Hampshire house of representatives in 1776, he gave up this post to represent his state in Philadelphia.

WILLIAM WHIPPLE   MATTHEW THORNTON

Saml Adams

John Adams

Robt Treat Paine

Elbridge Gerry

As William Ellery studied the next delegate to approach the table, he was reminded of some of the events that had culminated in this historic moment. Samuel Adams, known to many as the "firebrand of the Revolution," was a plain, unprepossessing man of medium build who dressed shabbily and appeared undistinguished in the company of so many wealthy delegates. But on close scrutiny, his penetrating steel-gray eyes revealed a man of unusual power. In business he had been a failure—he had no head for figures. But given an audience of concerned citizens he could charge the atmosphere in such a way as to arouse the most casual listener. From a distance men thought he was austere, yet in private gatherings he could be genial and entertaining. Sam Adams was born in Boston September 27, 1722, entered Harvard College, graduated from Harvard Law School, had tried his hand at becoming a merchant, and had finally turned to politics as the clamor for colonial rights began to stir the populace.

Here was the man, Ellery realized, who had led protests against the Stamp Tax, who had harangued crowds on the Boston water front, and who had organized the raiders who carried out the daring "Boston Tea Party," dumping chests of valuable tea into the waters of Boston harbor.

When he became clerk of the Massachusetts Assembly, he carried on a voluminous correspondence with patriot leaders in other colonies and in the course of this work he conceived the idea of setting up the "Committees of Correspondence." The plan was first put into operation in 1772 so that various groups in Massachusetts could keep each other advised of revolutionary activity. The idea spread rapidly through the colonies until it became a key factor in the unification of America.

Samuel Adams was one of the first leaders to suggest the formation of a Continental Congress. Long before most of the delegates to this congress were ready to accept the idea, Adams was speaking out for independence. He was a forceful, persuasive speaker but by no means a polished orator. His effectiveness was due to the depth of his conviction rather than to personality or eloquence.

Now, at fifty-four, he signed the document for which he had worked so hard. His hands shook, his eyes were watery, and his clothes were plain and ill-fitting. Yet here was one of the great architects of the American republic.

The other Adams was next in line. John, a second cousin of Sam Adams, was also a Harvard graduate. He was a native of the same town as John Hancock's birthplace— Braintree, Massachusetts—and was a leader in the patriot movement from its very beginnings when protests against the Stamp Act were being voiced in 1765. He was a powerful spokesman for independence, yet his keen legal mind was never clouded by prejudice or uncontrolled emotion. Even in the face of popular outrage, he defended British soldiers who had taken part in the "Boston Massacre," arguing at their murder trial that the true criminals were the supreme authorities in England, and that the troops were merely carrying out orders of their superiors. He won acquittal for all but two of the soldiers. The two were convicted of manslaughter and released without severe punishment.

This was a test of moral courage on the part of John Adams. He knew that he was risking his political career by defending the

SAMUEL ADAMS

soldiers, but as it turned out, the people of Massachusetts showed respect for his honesty and courage by electing him to the General Court, or legislature. From there, he went to the First Continental Congress, where he was prevailed upon by friends to restrain himself in expressing his views on independence. Though he was personally convinced that a break with England was inevitable, he went along with the more conservative delegates who believed that a formal protest to the British Government would suffice to bring the desired improvements. John and Samuel Adams, as well as a number of other delegates, including Patrick Henry and George Washington, bided their time, certain that they would be forced to fight.

At the Second Continental Congress, which convened May 10, 1775, it was John Adams who proposed that George Washington be

appointed commander-in-chief of the Continental Army. The army was organized, the forces for independence grew stronger, and the inevitable break with Britain came as John had predicted it would.

The next Massachusetts signer was a distinguished-looking gentleman with a strong, determined face. Robert Treat Paine had won a wide reputation for his eloquent speeches condemning Britain's highhanded policies in America. He was, at the signing, forty-five years old and was generally considered the foremost attorney of Massachusetts. His Puritan background had given him an unbending code of behavior. What he lacked in humor he made up for in determination, honor and courage. At the urging of his parents he had studied theology, served as a chaplain in a New England regiment, and for a time delivered sermons in Boston churches. For some unexplained reason, he shifted to a study of law, paying for his own

JOHN ADAMS

schooling by teaching on the side. Paine began his law practice about 1759 in Taunton, Massachusetts, where he married a Miss Sally Cobb. Then, as people began to protest against edicts of the British governor of Massachusetts, Robert Paine joined the patriots and attended meetings and conventions. By a curious coincidence, at the historic signing of the Declaration, he followed the man he had opposed at the trial of British soldiers in Boston, for it was Paine who had been appointed special prosecutor in that celebrated case. As a delegate to the Congress he won the sobriquet of the "Objector," due to his constant opposition to motions and proposals. Generally, he supported united colonial action in the hope that Britain would accede to their demands. He did not favor independence until the outbreak of actual fighting in 1775. Then he chaired a committee for the purchase of guns and bayonets.

Paine finally voted for the Declaration, and he signed it without hesitation despite his earlier moderate position.

William Ellery looked in vain for the last of the Massachusetts delegates, Elbridge Gerry, a slender young man of thirty-two, a native of Marblehead, who had worked for independence from the earliest days of patriot activity. Another Harvard graduate, Gerry was a close friend of Thomas Jefferson and John Adams. He was serious, intense, and given to switching his support from one group in Congress to another. Nevertheless, he had voted for the Declaration, and despite his apparent indecision on many issues, he consistently supported legislation to strengthen the armed forces and served on a number of committees involved in arming and equipping troops.

On August 2, the day of the formal signing, Gerry was absent from Congress. He did not put his signature to the document until November 19, 1776.

One of the elder delegates now stepped forward to sign the Declaration. He walked unsteadily, shuffling slowly to the table where he took up the quill in a hand that shook with palsy. This was Stephen Hopkins, sixty-nine, the signer who said, "My hand trembles, but my heart does not."

Hopkins had been involved in Rhode Island politics for nearly 50 years, having served in the Rhode Island legislature for many terms and having been elected governor of the colony nine times. Strongly in favor of the abolition of slavery, he had freed the slaves on his own estate. As early as 1759 Stephen Hopkins had advocated a union of the American colonies. As chief justice of the Rhode Island superior court he refused to have a group of colonists arrested after they burned a British revenue schooner, the *Gaspée,* in protest against restrictive Navigation Acts. From the beginning, Hopkins spoke vehemently in support of independence. He was one of the few delegates at the First Continental Congress who opposed any form of conciliation with Britain.

STEPHEN HOPKINS

The *Gaspée* burning
in Rhode Island waters

CONNECTICUT

Litchfield • • Hartford • Lebanon

Norwich •

• New Haven

Bridgeport •

The self-appointed observer, William Ellery, the other delegate from Rhode Island, had come to know Stephen Hopkins well. He admired the elder statesman for his unshakeable courage and conviction, and was proud to follow him to the table and to add his name to the parchment. Ellery was a much younger man, forty-eight on this occasion. He was a native of Newport, a Harvard graduate, and had entered into a number of business ventures without much success. Finally he became a lawyer, in which profession his keen wit was a valuable asset. He soon built up a large practice in Rhode Island and became so well known that he was overwhelmingly elected to the Continental Congress. Since Rhode Island had already declared its independence from Britain at the time Ellery took his seat in May 1776, he was naturally one of the foremost advocates of independence for all the colonies and he had pledged his large fortune to Congress. He was an odd-looking fellow, rather short and stockily built with a head that appeared too large. He loathed physical exercise, but devoted his energy to mental and intellectual pursuits. His caustic remarks often brought laughter to the serious debates in the State House. Now under Stephen Hopkins' shaky signature Ellery wrote his name with a neat, confident flourish, then returned to his place to observe the rest of the proceedings.

The next signer was Roger Sherman of Connecticut, a self-taught lawyer who had started his career as a shoemaker's apprentice. His father was a Massachusetts farmer who had little money for the boy's education. As a result Roger read dozens of books on politics, theology and law. Meanwhile he continued to repair shoes and did some surveying until he had acquired enough money to set up his own law office. His courage and determination were demonstrated when as a young man he moved from Newton, Massachusetts, to New Milford, Connecticut, walking over a hundred miles with a heavy case of shoemaker's tools strapped to his back. Not only did he learn law from his reading, but he became an accomplished mathematician. He used this knowledge in his work as a surveyor and he even delved into astronomy. Ultimately he moved to New Haven, Connecticut, where he became a popular leader in political affairs. He was elected to the Connecticut legislature, became a judge of the superior court, and defended colonial rights against the unpopular edicts of the British Parliament. Shortly before the Revolution he headed the New Haven Committee of Correspondence. He was a sober, plainly dressed Puritan who, according to Thomas Jefferson, "never said a foolish thing in his life." When he was only forty-five, Sherman held four positions at one time, serving on the governor's council, the Connecticut upper house, as judge of the Connecticut high court and as treasurer of Yale College. Having helped to draft the Declaration, he signed it

with a stiff, clear hand as plain and un-
complicated as his Yankee upbringing.

Sherman was followed by two other Connecticut delegates: Samuel Huntington and
William Williams. Huntington was a quiet
man, dignified and reserved in his manner,
and although he could scarcely be numbered
among the fiery patriots, he was firm in his

To the Hon.ble Jonathan Law Esqr. Govr. of CONNECTICUT in New-Engd. this Prospect of YALE COLLEGE is humbly dedicated by his Honour's most humble Servt. James Buck.

33

WILLIAM WILLIAMS

OLIVER WOLCOTT

Declaration of Independence.

William Williams, also age forty-five, next took up the quill pen. Here was another stern faced New Englander, son of a Congregationalist minister. Williams was a Harvard graduate who had at one time thought of following his father and grandfather into the ministry. However, during the French and Indian Wars, he served with his uncle, Colonel Ephraim Williams, the founder of Williams College, and he returned with a determination to become a merchant. In this he enjoyed some success, but his election to the Connecticut legislature in 1757 drew him into a lifelong political career. Sent as a delegate to the Second Continental Congress, he voted to break all ties with England. He pledged everything he had to the colonial cause, even signing promissory notes in 1775 to raise money for the army.

Another Connecticut delegate, Oliver Wolcott, did not sign the Declaration until September 4, as he had been forced to leave Philadelphia in June due to poor health. Nevertheless, he was an ardent patriot. It was Wolcott who had brought the New York statue of George III to his home in Windsor, Connecticut, where his wife and other ladies of the town melted it down to make bullets for the Continental Army. Wolcott was born in Windsor on November 20, 1726. He was as much a soldier as he was a politican; after graduating from Yale College with highest honors, he had accepted a captain's commission and fought on the northern frontier in the French and Indian War. He became a major general of the Connecticut militia and in 1776 he led fourteen regiments in the defense of New York City. This action prolonged his absence from Congress, but shortly after his units had joined with the main body of the Continental Army in New York, he returned to Philadelphia and added his signature to the Declaration.

belief that the colonies should be independent. Although he had held the post of King's attorney right up to the outbreak of revolution, he never faltered in his work for the patriot cause once the colonies had set their course toward independence. Like Roger Sherman, he was the son of a Puritan farmer and he had largely educated himself. He had first been apprenticed to a cooper where he learned to make barrels, but he studied law in his spare time and was admitted to the bar when he was twenty-seven. From a successful law practice he entered politics and served in the Connecticut legislature, then in the Second Continental Congress. He was forty-five when he signed the

The geographical order of delegates brought the New York representatives to the table next. The first of this group was William Floyd, a well-to-do young man of forty-one who had been active in community affairs on Long Island and was a major general in his local militia. His estate was particularly vulnerable to British seizure, for the redcoats had already occupied Staten Island in July and the number of British warships in New York harbor had been increasing daily until the masts of more than a hundred vessels were clustered like a leafless forest; their decks were crowded with the blue uniforms of German mercenaries and the scarlet of crack British units. Yet another enemy flo-

tilla appeared in the harbor, sailing in from the south almost at the time that William Floyd was signing the Declaration.

William Floyd was, therefore, well aware of the risk he took in supporting the patriot cause, yet he had thrown himself wholeheartedly into the struggle for independence. The son of a prosperous landowner, Floyd spent much of his boyhood and early youth in sport and social activities. What little education he received was largely from tutoring at home, but he was a logical thinker, and his consistent support of the patriot movement made him popular with the people in his community.

After Floyd had joined the Suffolk County militia, he rose to command of the unit. In 1774 he was chosen to represent New York at the First Continental Congress. He returned to his estate at a time when a British invasion of Long Island was threatened. Floyd immediately called his militia and prepared to fight any landings the British might attempt.

View of New York from the northwest shortly before 1773

However, the invasion did not take place. At the Second Continental Congress, he served on a number of committees. Although he favored independence, along with the other New York delegates, he abstained from voting on the Declaration, pending instructions from the New York legislature. New York's approval was voted in time for them to sign the document on August 2.

Floyd was followed by a much older gentleman, a stout, stern-looking man of sixty-two, who had been born at Livingston Manor, his family's huge estate in Albany and who had conducted a highly profitable business as an importer in New York City. Philip Livingston was as stern in his beliefs and principles as in appearance. His temper flared over any injustice and he had been angered by the arrogance of British rule. At the same time, he was opposed to violence on the part of overzealous patriots. Repeatedly he tried to inject reason into protests to the royal governor of New York, and when he was selected to serve in the colonial assembly in 1768 he led that body in drawing up a set of resolutions demanding that the British Parliament recognize certain rights of the colonies.

This action was premature. The governor dissolved the assembly, and in a new election, pro-British Tories won a popular majority. But the relations of the colonies with England continued to deteriorate, and Philip Livingston was sent to the First Continental Congress in 1774. He and his brothers, William and Robert, were also delegates to the Second Continental Congress, but William left Philadelphia to command the New Jersey militia prior to adoption of the Declaration, and Robert, opposing independence as too radical a step, withdrew from the Congress after serving briefly on the committee to draft the Declaration. Thus, of the three brothers, only Philip was on hand for the signing. Having

tried to restrain the colonists from taking this drastic step, he nevertheless joined with the majority when the final decision was made.

It was to be an ironical fact of history that Livingston and other New York signers who had at first been lukewarm to independence, were among the men who were to suffer most at the hands of British troops. One of these was sixty-three-year-old Francis Lewis, the next delegate to affix his signature to the Declaration. Lewis was one of eight signers who were born abroad. He was a native of Llandaff in Wales, was educated in London, and had come to America at the age of twenty-four. He had settled in New York City where he developed a successful merchandising firm and accumulated a comfortable fortune. After an adventurous career which included being shipwrecked on the coast of Ireland and being captured by Indians during the French and Indian Wars in 1756, he retired from business at the age of fifty-two, to devote his talents to public

PHILIP LIVINGSTON

service. Lewis quickly became a leader in protests against the British Stamp Tax and other restrictive laws. He was outspoken in his denunciation of pro-British colonists, yet he was slow to accept the idea of complete independence, believing as did many New Yorkers that Parliament could be persuaded to take a more moderate course. As it became obvious that no amount of reason could change royal policy, he took a firm stand on independence and signed the Declaration without the slightest hesitation. For this he and his family were destined to pay a heavy price.

Last to sign for the New York delegation was Lewis Morris, age fifty. William Ellery saw him as an aristocratic gentleman with the proud bearing of a man who had been born to affluence. A grandson of the first royal governor of New Jersey, he had inherited "Morrisania," an estate of over two thousand acres covering a large area of what is now the Bronx in New York City. While most of his wealthy neighbors were Tories who supported British policy, Morris spoke out forcefully against England, and after making some fiery speeches in the New York Assembly, he was soon deeply involved in patriot activity. He worked with George Washington on plans for supplying a continental army, and was sent on a mission to western Pennsylvania in order to gain support of Indians in fighting the British.

In 1776, he was elected to serve in the Second Continental Congress, but as he was also a brigadier general of New York militia, his military duties kept him away from Philadelphia during the debates over the Declaration. However he was on hand for the signing on August 2. Tall, distinguished, and immaculately dressed, the fifty-year-old Morris stepped forward, took the quill and put his huge fortune on the line with a few strokes of the pen and a bold calligraphic flourish.

As the first of New Jersey's delegates moved to the table, William Ellery watched him with intense interest. Here was another man of considerable means, but one who had been known as a moderate, and who had at first resisted drastic measures in dealing with Britain. Richard Stockton, forty-five, a graduate of the College of New Jersey, wealthy landowner and successful lawyer, had been won over to the side of independence. He showed not the slightest hesitation in signing his name to the Declaration. If he had any premonition of the personally disastrous consequences of his act, he gave no sign of it as Ellery observed him.

Stockton's background could easily have led him to a Tory viewpoint. While serving as a trustee of the College of New Jersey he had gone to Scotland in 1766 for the purpose of finding a new president for the college. It was on this mission that he met John Witherspoon, and prevailed upon him to accept the college presidency. After his return to America, Stockton was asked to serve on the executive council of William Franklin, the royal governor of New Jersey. In this position he was surrounded by conservatives and loyalists to whom colonial independence was unthinkable. Stockton was naturally influenced by these men, and for a time he had believed that reconciliation between Britain and the colonies was possible. However, when it became clear that a break with England was inevitable he resigned from the governor's council. He was appointed to the supreme court of New Jersey in 1774, and

to the Continental Congress in June 1776, just in time for him to hear John Adams' plea for the Declaration of Independence. By this time he was wholeheartedly dedicated to the patriot cause.

The somberly dressed clergyman who followed Richard Stockton to the table was the Rev. John Witherspoon, the Scottish Presbyterian pastor, whom Stockton had brought to America in 1768 as the newly appointed president of the College of New Jersey — later Princeton University. Witherspoon was born in 1723 near Edinburgh and was a descendant of the great founder of Protestantism in Scotland, John Knox. Witherspoon entered Edinburgh University at the age of fourteen, graduated at eighteen, but continued to study theology for another three years. After accepting the pastorate of a parish in Beith, he became involved with the people in their attempts to restore "Bonnie Prince Charlie" to the throne. He was captured by English troops at the Battle of Falkirk in 1746, but was released after a brief term in prison. He rapidly gained a wide reputation for his writings on individual rights and human dignity. When Richard Stockton sought to bring him to America, Elizabeth Witherspoon, his wife, objected because she feared that life in the colonial "wilderness" would be too rugged for her and their five children. But a mutual friend, Benjamin Rush, an American who was studying medicine at Edinburgh at the time, joined Stockton in persuading the couple to go.

Witherspoon's direction of the College of New Jersey was highly successful. He quickly became a leading figure in colonial affairs, siding with the revolutionary groups from the beginning. During a debate over the course the colonies should take he once heard a remark that America was not yet ripe for a declaration of independence. He was reported to have replied, "In my judgment, we are

h-West Prospect of Nassau-Hall, with a Fr... *...New Jersey,*

JOHN WITHERSPOON

not only ripe for independence, but in danger of rotting for want of it." He needed no persuasion to vote for and then sign the Declaration.

In direct contrast to the dignified Reverend Witherspoon was Francis Hopkinson, an energetic little man with a lively manner and a habit of speaking in short, rapid sentences. Although he was a native of Philadelphia, where he was born in 1737, Hopkinson had settled in Bordentown, New Jersey, after his marriage to Ann Borden, a wealthy heiress.

His growing reputation as a lawyer brought him an appointment to the New Jersey governor's council. Nevertheless he supported the patriots and wrote such scathing articles about British rule that he soon had a large and enthusiastic following in the colonies.

Hopkinson's father, Thomas, had been a well-to-do lawyer and jurist, and was the American Philosophical Society's first president when the organization was founded in 1744. Young Francis had been educated at the College of Philadelphia (later to become

the University of Pennsylvania) and was a member of its first graduating class. He then studied law at the office of Benjamin Chew, attorney general of Pennsylvania.

Hopkinson visited England when he was twenty-eight, lived at his uncle's home for several months and met some of the most important British leaders, including the prime minister. Much as he enjoyed his stay, he returned to America with no great affection for Britain's rulers, and by the time the Second Continental Congress convened, Hopkinson was eager to serve in it.

"Honest John Hart," a plainly dressed Jersey farmer, was the next delegate to sign. Hart, now sixty-five, had been a tall, dark-haired youth whose good looks and good manners had endeared him to his neighbors. Although he had received a meager education, his honesty, hard work and common sense had marked him as a leader in his community. He had been born in Stonington, Connecticut, in 1711, but had been brought to New Jersey by his parents when he was a small boy. His life had been quiet and productive. His 380-acre farm prospered, and his wife, Deborah, presented him with 13 children. As a justice of the peace for Hunterdon County, he won a reputation for fair dealing, and in 1761 was elected to the New Jersey legislature. While serving on that body he voted opposition to the British Stamp Act and backed the refusal to pay British troops stationed in the colony. In 1774 he served as a member of the first congress called by New Jersey to elect delegates to the newly formed Continental Congress.

Because the original New Jersey delegation in Philadelphia opposed independence, the provincial legislature had voted to replace it with a new group, which included John Hart. As a result he was on hand August 2 to sign the Declaration and, like Richard Stockton, was destined to suffer tragic consequences.

Abraham Clark was the last of the New Jersey delegates to come forward. William Ellery saw a man of fifty, rather stout, dignified, with an expression of solemn determination. Born in Elizabethtown, New Jersey, in 1726, he had been a frail child whose parents considered him too sickly to be sent to school. He taught himself mathematics and the fundamentals of law. Although he had never been admitted to the bar, he offered free legal advice to the poor and as a result he earned the nickname of "The Poor Man's Counselor." An early champion of independence, he joined the New Jersey Committee of Safety in 1774, and when in June 1776, the state legislature arrested and imprisoned the royal governor, William Franklin, Clark was selected as one of the new patriot delegates to the Second Continental Congress. Along with the other New Jersey representatives he had voted for independence and adoption of the Declaration. Now, only a month after his arrival in Philadelphia, he was affixing his signature to the all-important document.

View of Philadelphia from the Jersey shore in 1768

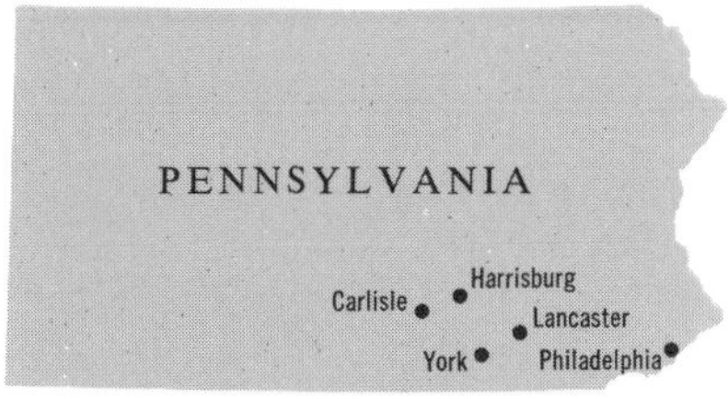

PENNSYLVANIA

Carlisle • • Harrisburg
• Lancaster
York • • Philadelphia

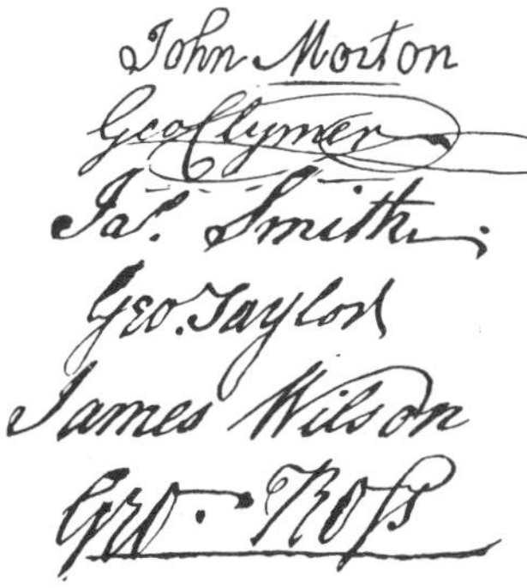

Robt Morris
Benjamin Rush
Benj. Franklin

John Morton
Geo Clymer
Ja^s. Smith
Geo. Taylor
James Wilson
Geo. Ross

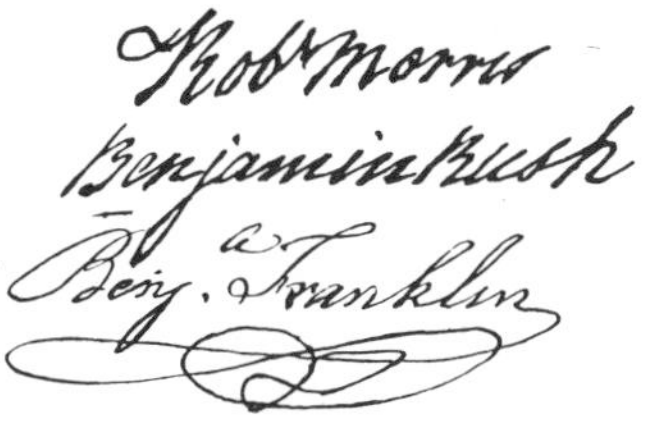

The man who became the "Financier of the Revolution," and who was first of the Pennsylvania delegates to sign the Declaration, was Robert Morris, forty-two, a Philadelphia merchant who had cautiously abstained from voting for independence from Great Britain. Despite his early opposition to the Stamp Tax and his membership in the Philadelphia Committee of Safety, he had steadfastly opposed violence or any drastic action against British authority. He was born in Liverpool, England, in 1734, the son of a prosperous tobacco merchant who came to Maryland when Robert was still a young boy. He was sent to school in Philadelphia, and it was in that city that he learned the import business with the well-established trading firm of Charles Willing. After his father was accidentally killed by a cannon that was firing a salute to the arrival of one of

ROBERT MORRIS

the College at the age of fourteen. Young as he was, he took up the study of medicine under a Philadelphia doctor by the name of Redman. For six grueling years he worked with Redman, gaining much practical experience during one of the terrible yellow fever epidemics of that period. Then, in 1776, he sailed to England and continued his medical studies at the University of Edinburgh, Scotland. While there, he learned of his uncle's death, and was asked by Richard Stockton and other trustees of the College of New Jersey to speak to John Witherspoon about the vacant position at the College. It was partly due to Rush's persuasive arguments that Witherspoon finally accepted the post. Ultimately, they became fellow signers of the Declaration. Benjamin Rush, Richard Stockton and John Witherspoon all became fast friends, and Rush married Stockton's daughter, Julia, in 1776.

In London, Dr. Rush met Benjamin Franklin, who took such a liking to him that he made a 200-pound loan to the young physician for a trip to Paris. Rush spent much of his time in the French capital visiting hospitals and studying their facilities. After returning to Philadelphia, he won considerable fame not only as a leading physician but as a brilliant essayist on independence from Britain. In 1769 he became a professor of chemistry at the College of Philadelphia.

Elected to the Second Continental Congress in July 1776, he was seated too late to vote for the Declaration, but on August 2 he signed with genuine enthusiasm.

Now Ellery leaned slightly forward to watch the oldest member of the Congress who stepped to the table and took up the quill. Following the thirty-year-old Benjamin Rush, Dr. Franklin at seventy looked old indeed, and his silvered hair and his spectacles gave him an air of venerable dignity. Everyone loved and respected Benjamin

his ships, Robert Morris worked diligently in the Philadelphia company, becoming a full-fledged partner at the age of twenty. The firm, which became known as Willing, Morris & Company, was one of the leading shipping concerns in the colonies. Elected to the Pennsylvania legislature late in 1775, Morris was picked as one of that body's representatives in the Continental Congress, where he became a member of a vital committee to obtain arms from foreign countries. He also took part in laying plans for building an American navy. However, he did not appear for the vote on independence on July 2, or for the adoption of the Declaration two days later. He continued to argue that the colonies were not ready to break away from England; still, he signed the Declaration with a firm hand.

Morris was followed by the young physician, Benjamin Rush, who had played an important role in persuading John Witherspoon to accept the presidency of the College of New Jersey. From his station near the table, William Ellery saw a handsome fellow of thirty, and he marvelled at this youthful delegate's accomplishments. A native of Philadelphia, Rush had received his early education at his uncle's West Nottingham Academy in Maryland. The uncle, Samuel Finley, was later appointed president of the College of New Jersey, and Rush followed him there as a student. He graduated from

Franklin. When he took up the pen to inscribe his famous name on the parchment, all conversation in the hall ceased for a moment. He had already become such a giant of his time, that his connection with the Declaration seemed overshadowed by so many previous accomplishments.

Franklin had been born in Boston, January 17, 1706, the youngest son of a candlemaker by the name of Josiah Franklin. Ben had learned the printing trade largely because his parents were unable to afford the education necessary for him to become what they hoped would be his calling — that of a minister. After a five-year apprenticeship in his brother James' print shop, at the age of seventeen, Benjamin took passage on a ship to New York. He was now an established journalist, for unknown to James, he had been writing essays for his brother's newspaper, signing them, "Mrs. Silence Dogood." When Ben failed to find work in New York, he went on to Philadelphia where he obtained a job as a printer's assistant. While thus employed, he rented a room in the house of Deborah Read, whom he later married. A year or so afterward, the governor of Pennsylvania, Sir William Keith, took an interest in young Franklin, offered to set him up in business with a printing shop, and urged him to go to London to buy presses and type. Keith assured Franklin that he would send letters of credit to finance the enterprise. But after he arrived in England in 1725, Franklin found that Governor Keith had not lived up to his promise. Forced to find work with a London printer, Franklin spent eighteen months enjoying life in the British metropolis. Then a wealthy Philadelphia merchant, who was in London on business, met Franklin and persuaded him to return to America and to work for him in his shipping firm. Back in Philadelphia, he spent only a brief period in Thomas Denham's business, then returned to printing when the merchant died. Franklin began to save his money for the purpose of acquiring his own shop. He founded the Junto, a philosophical club, from which grew the American Philosophical Society. At the same time, he built up the Junto's library and in 1731 he used this as the basis for the first circulating library — the Library Company of Philadelphia. Mean-

Left to right

JOHN MORTON

GEORGE CLYMER

JAMES SMITH

GEORGE TAYLOR

JAMES WILSON

while, in 1729, he began publishing *The Pennsylvania Gazette* with the help of a printer partner, Hugh Meredith. Three years later, in 1732, he established *Poor Richard's Almanack*. This quickly became the leading American periodical with its witty commentary and maxims. When he was thirty, Franklin became a clerk in the legislature of Pennsylvania. This began for him a political career that included such offices as postmaster of Philadelphia (later of the colonies), representative in the Pennsylvania legislature and delegate to the Continental Congress. Meanwhile his scientific experiments led to the invention of the famous Franklin stove, bifocal glasses, an electric storage battery, and to the discovery that lightning was an electrical charge.

As early as 1754, when the French and Indian Wars threatened American security, Franklin outlined a plan for uniting the colonies under a representative government, but the plan was never adopted.

Franklin spent five years in London representing Pennsylvania in a tax dispute between the colonists and the "proprietors" of Pennsylvania who were descended from William Penn. The British proprietors claimed tax exemption for their lands, but Franklin won his case for the colony. The tax exemption was withdrawn for all but land that had never been surveyed. On a later visit to London in 1765, he worked successfully for repeal of the Stamp Act, but this unpopular tax measure had permanently damaged relations between Britain and the American colonies. Franklin continued to serve in England as a diplomatic representative of Pennsylvania, Georgia, New Jersey and Massachusetts. Despite his wise council, British authorities took an increasingly dim view of Franklin's efforts to present the colonial viewpoint, and with war imminent, he returned to America, arriving May 5, 1775.

He was promptly elected to the Continental Congress, served on the Pennsylvania Committee of Safety, and was appointed Postmaster General of the colonies.

Having helped Jefferson to draft the Declaration of Independence, he now signed it with an elaborate flourish.

After the great Dr. Franklin came John Morton, a fifty-two-year-old delegate from Ridley Township, near the town of Chester, Pennsylvania. Joining with Franklin and James Wilson, he had cast the deciding Pennsylvania vote for independence on July 2, the day when John Dickinson and Robert Morris were absent and when Charles Humphreys and Thomas Willing voted against the Declaration. His key support of independence turned many of his friends and neighbors against him, since there were many loyalist Quakers in his community.

Morton was born in 1724, the son of John and Mary Richards Morton. The father died before the birth of his son, and as a result John Junior was brought up by a stepfather, John Sketchley, who taught the boy surveying and mathematics. At thirty-two Morton was elected to the Pennsylvania legislature, on which he served for over 20 years. He strongly opposed British tax policies, a stand that made him a popular figure throughout the colony. For three years he served as sheriff of Delaware County, was elected speaker of the house of representatives, then became an associate judge of the Pennsylvania supreme court. When he was sent to the First Continental Congress in 1774, he worked for healing the rift with Britain, but in the Second Congress he began to support the independence movement.

John Morton was followed by a much younger man, George Clymer, thirty-seven, a Philadelphia merchant who had been working diligently for the break from England. Clymer, a partner in the shipping

firm of Meredith and Clymer, was a close friend of George Washington. He was reserved, quiet, but thoroughly informed on the trends and events of his time. After graduation from the College of Philadelphia he had learned the importing business in the counting house of his uncle, William Coleman. At twenty-six he married Elizabeth Meredith, daughter of another prosperous Philadelphian who took him into the firm as a partner. Early in the period of tension with Great Britain, Clymer took an active part in the colonial cause, attending protest meetings and speaking in defense of colonial rights. He joined the local militia, became a captain, and was elected to the Pennsylvania Committee of Safety. When the Continental Congress began to seek funds for the army, George Clymer was appointed treasurer with the task of raising money to support Washington. He exchanged all of his personal assets for Continental paper money and prevailed upon most of his wealthy friends and business acquaintances to follow suit. When the Pennsylvania delegation to Congress expressed opposition to independence, several delegates were recalled and replaced by popular demand, and among the new appointees was George Clymer. He took his seat July 20, 1776, too late to vote for the Declaration, but just in time to sign the historic document.

Next of the Pennsylvania delegates was James Smith, Irish born son of a York County farmer who had settled in Pennsylvania in 1729. Like George Clymer, he had attended the College of Philadelphia, and had been elected to the Congress as a replacement for anti-independence delegates on the same date as Clymer. Smith's career had previously been devoted largely to law and surveying. Not until 1774 did he become involved in politics. His conviction that war with England was inevitable led him to organize the first Pennsylvania Company of patriot troops, and

he was elected its captain. Shortly afterward he became colonel of a full regiment. In 1775 and 1776 Smith served as a delegate to patriot conventions, and was finally sent to the Second Continental Congress on July 20, 1776, in time to join in the signing, August 2.

Smith was followed closely by George Taylor, another Irish immigrant. Taylor was a comparative unknown to Ellery and other veterans of the Continental Congress. He had come to America when he was about twenty-one, an indentured servant who had been forced to earn his freedom by hard work in an iron foundry near Durham, Pennsylvania. When it became clear that he was not strong enough to endure the strenuous furnace stoking, he became the firm's bookkeeper. Eventually, he married his employer's widow, Anne Taylor Savage, became the owner of the foundry and built up a large and prosperous business. With the spread of revolutionary fever in the colonies, Taylor accepted the commission of colonel in the local militia and was elected to the Pennsylvania legislature in 1775, an outspoken patriot who urged a full break with England. Now, at the age of sixty, as one of the five replacement delegates who had joined Congress on July 20, he proudly signed his name to the Declaration.

The next Pennsylvania signer was better known to William Ellery, who knew him as one of the most scholarly men in America. James Wilson was born in Scotland, had received his education at the universities of Glasgow, St. Andrews, and Edinburgh. When he was only twenty-three he decided to find a career in America, and he arrived in New York some time in 1765 when the first rumblings of discontent were being heard in the colonies. Wilson found employment as a Latin teacher at the College of Philadelphia. Shortly afterward he began a study of law in the firm of John Dickinson. Wilson lived for a time in Carlisle, Pennsylvania, where he

New Castle

Dover

DELAWARE

Caesar Rodney

Geo Read

Tho M:Kean

practiced law and married Rachel Bird. During this period, between 1767 and 1775, he became recognized as an outstanding patriot writer. His pamphlet, *Considerations of the Nature and Extent of the Legislative Authority of the British Parliament,* had wide circulation and was probably a factor in winning him election to the Second Continental Congress in 1775. Although his legal tutor, John Dickinson, opposed the Declaration, Wilson voted for it, and he proudly inscribed his name to the parchment on August 2. He was one of the younger signers, only thirty-three at the time.

Finally, George Ross signed for the Pennsylvania delegation. Ross was a real veteran of the Congress, having been a delegate to the First Continental Congress as well as the Second. In the earlier period he had been a loyalist, voting opposition to drastic action against England. Ross was of Scottish descent, but had been born in New Castle, Delaware, the son of an Episcopal minister. When the senior George Ross became assistant rector of Christ Church in Philadelphia, the family moved to Pennsylvania, and it was in Philadelphia that young Ross grew up and received most of his education. He studied law, and was admitted to the bar in 1750, at the age of twenty. He practiced law in Lancaster, Pennsylvania, and in 1768 was elected to the Pennsylvania legislature. His conservative views gradually changed as Britain continued to show its disdain for colonial petitions. Though not at first a delegate to the Second Continental Congress, he worked tirelessly for the Pennsylvania Committee of Safety, helped to draft the Pennsylvania State Constitution, and was chosen as one of the five replacements for the anti-independence delegates to the Congress. His tall, distinctive script at the bottom of the large list of Pennsylvania signatures stands out boldly as testimony that his earlier caution had been tossed aside.

William Ellery, his chin on his hand, was studying the countenance of the next signer. Caesar Rodney, the first of the Delaware delegation to come to the table, had won the eternal admiration of his Congressional associates with his wild ride from Dover, Delaware, on the night of July 1. Ellery found this man's appearance fascinating. Rodney was tall and thin. His small, wrinkled face seemed even smaller because of the green scarf he used to cover the left cheek that was afflicted by an advanced case of skin cancer. Despite his ill health, his eyes blazed with an indomitable spirit and a keen sense of humor. Born near Dover October 7, 1728, Caesar Rodney had been raised on his father's prosperous plantation. The father had died when Caesar was still a small boy, but his mother, acting as his tutor, had trained him to manage their large estate. At thirty he was elected sheriff of his county, became justice of the peace at the end of his term, and in 1761 was elected to the colonial legislature. In 1765 he was sent to the Stamp Act Congress in New York City.

Throughout his service in the Delaware legislature, Rodney supported the most liberal acts. He voted to prohibit the importation of slaves into Delaware, but the act was defeated. As speaker of the lower house of the legislature, he worked tirelessly for the patriot cause and was ultimately given chairmanship of the patriot convention. The convention elected him to the First and Second Continental Congresses.

The long night ride from Dover
to Philadelphia to vote for Independence

Smallest of the colonies after Rhode Island, Delaware represented an important link between the north and the south. Unfortunately loyalists were everywhere, especially in the vicinity of Dover, and as the independence movement had gained momentum, so had violent opposition to it among Delaware's Tories.

In an effort to combat this opposition, Caesar Rodney was recalled from Congress in 1775 and given the task of building up a powerful and well-drilled force of volunteers. This was, to say the least, a difficult assignment. Patriots with sufficient enthusi-

asm to leave their farms or their trades and professions to prepare for war with local Tories — many of whom were friends and neighbors — were hard to find. Yet Rodney set to work with his usual energy. He not only enlisted the required number of troops but within six months had made them one of the best disciplined units in all the colonies. Their presence alone helped to keep Tory activity to a minimum during 1775 and early 1776.

Nevertheless, the situation continued to be so tense that Rodney had been prevented from joining the debate over independence in

47

Philadelphia. Reports continued to circulate that an armed uprising in Delaware was imminent. Meanwhile Rodney had been commissioned a brigadier general to take command of the Delaware militia. It was because his military duties had kept him in Dover that his associate Thomas McKean had to summon him to the crucial vote in Congress on July 2. By voting for independence and signing the Declaration, Rodney knew that he had sealed his own death warrant, though not for the reason that he was guilty of treason in the eyes of Britain's rulers. His was a more personal problem, hopeless of solution. He had planned to go to London where a famous surgeon might have been able to save him. Now such a trip would be impossible, and there was no one in the colonies who knew how to treat his ailment.

The next signature to the Declaration is that of George Read. When he picked up the quill on August 2, 1776, he was forty-two years old, a cool, dignified jurist whose austere manner sometimes awed his compatriots. William Ellery, like most of the other delegates, had found him difficult to approach. He seemed to frown on familiarity and, as a result, had few close friends. Though he was a native of Maryland, he had studied law in Philadelphia and had set up his practice in New Castle, Delaware. A member of the colonial assembly of the Three Lower Counties, (originally administered by the governor of Pennsylvania) he took a strong stand against the Stamp Act, but was more cautious in his views on independence. His opposition to the Declaration prompted Thomas McKean to summon Rodney in order to provide the tie-breaking vote. Nevertheless, he signed the document with a firm, neat hand, and as far as Ellery could see he evinced neither doubt nor regret in taking this action.

Thomas McKean, the third and last representative of the newly formed state of Delaware was a forty-two-year-old lawyer from New Castle County. One of the most ardent patriots in the State House, tall, handsome Thomas McKean had been a fighter for freedom for the past 15 years, yet unfortunately he was not on hand to sign the Declaration on August 2. He was elected to the Delaware legislature in 1762, and he had served on this lawmaking body ever since. Delaware had sent him to the Stamp Act Congress in New York in 1765. On the basis of McKean's recommendation that each colony represented at the Stamp Act Congress have one vote, the equal voice rule was not only applied there, but in the Continental Congresses, and would be applied later in the Senate of the United States. During that same year of 1765, McKean became a justice of the peace in the court of common pleas in New Castle County. Under his jurisdiction, this court was the first in America to ignore the Stamp Act and to use unstamped documents in the conduct of its business. McKean was becoming increasingly popular in his community. In 1772 he was elected speaker of the Delaware house of representatives. He was then sent to the First Continental Congress, while he continued to serve as a delegate to the Delaware legislature and as a militia colonel for the state. In the Second Continental Congress, Thomas McKean favored independence from the very beginning of discussions on this explosive issue. William Ellery, watching for this ardent patriot, was disappointed not to see him in the gathering. When he inquired of a fellow delegate, he learned that McKean was absent on a tour of military duty with Washington's forces in New Jersey. McKean was not in a position to sign the Declaration until much later — probably some time in 1781. Although the exact date of his signing is not known, it is generally believed that he was the last of the delegates to affix his name to the document.

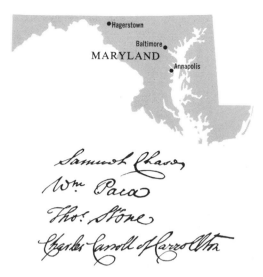

MARYLAND

SAMUEL CHASE

A heavyset gentleman led the four-man Maryland delegation to the table. He was Samuel Chase, who had been described by a leading citizen of Annapolis as "a busy, restless incendiary, a ringleader of mobs, a foulmouthed and inflaming son of discord and faction. . . a promoter of the lawless excesses of the multitude."* Chase was indeed a fiery patriot and a hot-tempered, argumentative politician. His florid face became easily reddened in the heat of debate. He was given to table- or desk-pounding as he spoke, and his Maryland compatriots nicknamed him "Bacon Face." Chase was only thirty-five when he signed the Declaration. He looked older. Ellery was amused by the angry expression on the Maryland delegate's face as he picked up the quill. Unlike the calm deliberation of the majority of signers, Chase wrote his name as though he wished the ink were pure venom that could somehow bring death to King George.

Samuel Chase was born on April 17, 1741 in Somerset County, Maryland. His father, Thomas Chase, was an Episcopal minister who became rector of St. Paul's Church in Baltimore. Under his father's tutelage, Samuel received a classical education, but as his mother had died at his birth, he apparently lacked training in gentlemanly manners. In 1759 he undertook the study of law in Annapolis, and he was admitted to the bar in 1761. Shortly afterward, when he was only

* Whitney, David C., Founders of Freedom in America, Chicago, Ill., J. G. Ferguson Publishing Company, 1964, p. 63.

twenty-three, he was elected to the Maryland legislature. From the start of his political career he showed his opposition to the royal governor and to external British rule. When the Stamp Act was passed in 1765, Chase led violent mob actions in protest, and burned in effigy the local stamp distributor, a royal agent. At the same time, he openly criticized other Maryland citizens and legislators for not being more outspoken in denouncing the tax.

After Chase took part in organizing the Maryland Committee of Correspondence, he was sent to the First Continental Congress where he was one of the few delegates to speak out passionately for rebellion against the Crown. In the Second Continental Congress he was pleased by the swing toward independence, and he was sent on a mission to Canada, along with Benjamin Franklin, John Carroll and Charles Carroll, in an effort to persuade the Canadians to break away from England. Since the mission failed, as did an abortive military expedition into Canada, Chase returned to Philadelphia in time to join in the debate over independence. To his dismay, he found that his own Maryland delegation had been instructed to vote *against* independence. He and Charles Carroll therefore took horses and rode to Maryland to address the legislature at Annapolis. They also travelled throughout the colony, making impromptu speeches in villages and on planta-

tions, urging the people to support the independence movement. So successful was this campaign that patriotic fervor swept Maryland. As a result, the legislature reversed its position and on June 28, Chase wrote a letter to John Adams saying, "I am just this moment from the house to procure an express to follow the post, with an unanimous vote of our convention for independence."*

Chase then mounted his horse and in a wild day-and-night ride, managed to arrive in Philadelphia in time to vote for independence with the other Maryland delegates on July 2.

William Paca followed Samuel Chase to the table. In contrast, here was a man of quiet dignity whose calm, legalistic appraisal of situations won the respect and confidence of his associates. Paca was born in Abingdon, Maryland, October 31, 1740, the son of John Paca, a wealthy plantation owner. After completing academic studies at the College of Philadelphia, he studied law in Annapolis and then in London. On his return to Annapolis, he set up a thriving law practice, married an heiress by the name of Mary Chew, and soon became a leader in his community. In 1768 he won election to the Maryland legislature where he became a close political ally of Samuel Chase. Although they were of entirely different temperaments, both men strongly opposed British efforts to rule by proclamation, and both took an early stand for independence. On one occasion, Paca and Chase led a crowd to the public square where they conducted a mock "hanging" of a governor's proclamation of taxes to be imposed on the colony. The proclamation was then buried under the gallows in solemn ceremony. Paca was appointed a delegate to the First Continental Congress in 1774, and to the Second Continental Congress a year later. He again worked closely with Samuel Chase during the campaign to pressure the Maryland legislature into releasing their delegates for an affirmative vote on independence. As a result, Paca was permitted to vote for the Declaration which he now proudly signed.

The next signer from Maryland, Thomas Stone, was one of the younger delegates. At thirty-three, he was tall and lean, and his face had the pallor of a serious scholar. He was born on his father's plantation in Charles County, Maryland, some time in 1743. The exact date is not recorded. He learned horsemanship at an early age, since he had to ride 20 miles to school every day. As a younger brother, he inherited nothing of his father's large estate, but he acquired a loan so that he could study law under Thomas Johnson in Annapolis. By the time he was twenty-one he had passed his bar examination and was practicing law in Frederick. Ironically, he was appointed by the Maryland government to prosecute patriots who were defying the tax laws, although his sympathies were with his fellow colonists. When he was sent to the Second Continental Congress in 1775, he tried to pursue a moderate course in respect to England, but as it became evident that independence was the only honorable solution to the colonial problem, he voted with the majority and was on hand for the historic signing on August 2. Quiet and undemonstrative, he was not well known to the delegates from other states.

Better known to William Ellery and to others in the hall was Charles Carroll, thirty-eight, who now accepted the quill pen from Thomas Stone. Carroll was the sole Roman Catholic in the Congress, a fact that intrigued Ellery, who knew that according to old Maryland law, Catholics were not permitted to enter politics. Consequently, Carroll's desire for independence and freedom from the old regime had been stirred not only by the usual motives but by a personal determination to

* Whitney, David C., Founders of Freedom in America, p. 65.

bring genuine religious freedom to Maryland. Not that the Carroll family had suffered privation. Their estate at Carrollton Manor and their other tracts were among the great land holdings in America; their wealth and position could be traced through their ancestry to ancient Irish royalty. Charles Carroll, the younger, was born in Annapolis on September 19, 1737. At the age of eight, his father took him to France where he received his early education from Jesuit fathers at a school in St. Omer. Because of the religious and educational restrictions against Roman Catholics in Maryland, the senior Charles Carroll attempted to acquire a tract of land in French Louisiana where he proposed to resettle American Catholics, but he was unsuccessful in this mission. Meanwhile, young Charles continued advanced studies in Paris and Rheims, then he took up the study of law at the Inner Temple in London. He returned to Maryland in 1764, fluent in the French language and with the manners of a European aristocrat. When his father presented him with the huge Carrollton Manor plantation, he became known as Charles Carroll of Carrollton, as distinguished from the elder Charles Carroll of Annapolis. He married his cousin, Mary Darnall, at a time when he was becoming an active participant in the patriot movement. Unable to seek a seat in the Maryland legislature, he wrote newspaper articles and pamphlets which he signed "Second Citizen." His theme was the illegality of law by proclamation, and his writings became so popular that citizens of Annapolis gratefully awarded him the title of Maryland's "First Citizen." More than any other leader in Maryland, and for good reason, Carroll spoke forthrightly for revolution and a clean break with England. It is said that he once debated this point even with the fiery patriot Samuel Chase. When Chase stated that the colonists had already won their points against the British with sound written arguments, Carroll is reported to have replied, "And do you think that writing will settle the question between us?" "Certainly," replied Chase. "What else can we resort to?" "The bayonet!" exclaimed Carroll without hesitation.

Carroll soon became active on Maryland's Committee of Safety and Committee of Correspondence. Early in 1775 he became a member of a "Committee of Observation," an unofficial but powerful ruling body that ignored royal decrees and took Maryland law into its own hands. Though he still could not legally be elected to the Continental Congress, he was nevertheless chosen by the Philadelphia body to accompany Benjamin Franklin, Samuel Chase, and Carroll's own cousin, John Carroll, on the mission to Canada in hope of enlisting Canadians in the fight for independence from England. On his return from this unsuccessful expedition he worked tirelessly to get the Maryland legislature's approval of the Declaration of Independence. Finally, on July 4, 1776, the day of the Declaration's adoption, the Maryland state convention appointed him to the Continental Congress. He arrived at the State House on July 18 and was thus on hand for the signing. As Carroll came forward, William Ellery heard someone remark, "There goes another fortune!" Carroll smiled and inscribed with a flourish, *"Charles Carroll of Carrollton."*

51

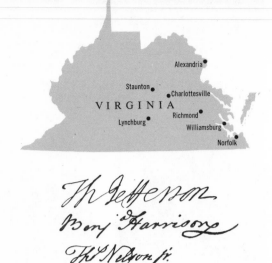

No other group of delegates had been more influential in bringing about the break with England than the gentlemen from Virginia. In fact, of all the 13 colonies, Virginia stood out boldly as the leader in revolutionary thought and action. Here were the men who conceived of American independence as a legal right which sprang from the illegality of foreign tyranny, and who saw individual freedom as a God-given, inalienable right common to all peoples. Curiously, most Virginians had not applied such advanced thinking to the subject of Negro slavery, but the principles they expounded were nonetheless sound, and their concepts transcended their own narrow application of them. First of the Virginia signers to come under William Ellery's observation was Thomas Jefferson, author of the Declaration of Independence. The sandy-haired, thirty-three-year-old delegate signed his own composition in a large, stiff hand as he leaned down over the table from his six-feet-two-inch height.

Jefferson's cool courage, his candor and his inflexible determination to build a nation of free and independent states had won universal admiration and respect among his associates. Though he possessed a quiet dignity, he was warm and cordial to his friends and was known to have remarked, "My habit is to speak only of men's good qualities."

Born April 13, 1743, Jefferson had grown up on his father's plantation in Albemarle County, Virginia, and had attended a local school where he studied Latin, Greek and other liberal arts subjects. At age fourteen, upon his father's death, he fell heir to a huge estate comprising over two thousand acres and about three dozen slaves. At seventeen he entered William and Mary College in Williamsburg, Virginia, graduating two years later, in 1762. He then undertook a study of law with George Wythe who was destined to become a fellow signer of the Declaration. Jefferson was an enthusiastic student of contemporary politics. He spent considerable time at the Virginia House of Burgesses, listening to the speeches and forming his own ideas of how a government should operate. When he heard Patrick Henry lash out against the Stamp Act, he was deeply affected by Henry's eloquence. For a few years Jefferson practiced law in Williamsburg, earning a comfortable income. During this time he also earned the reputation of being a radical thinker, for his views on individual freedom often clashed with the slave-owning members of his society. He won a seat in the Virginia House of Burgesses in 1769 and continued to serve on this body until the Revolution.

In 1772, Jefferson married Martha Wayles Skelton, a wealthy widow whose land holdings equalled his own. During this period he had begun the building of his famous home, Monticello, and he and his bride moved into the partially completed mansion.

As the colonies began to talk of open rebellion against England, Jefferson became a close friend of Richard Henry Lee, Patrick Henry, and Francis Lightfoot Lee. These three, together with Jefferson and his brother-in-law, Dabney Carr, held meetings at the Raleigh Tavern in Williamsburg. There they formed a Virginia Committee of Correspondence, and because the others recognized Jefferson's writing ability, they asked him to draw up appropriate resolutions which Carr presented to the House of Burgesses. On the prompt passage of the resolutions, Jefferson

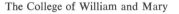

The College of William and Mary

THOMAS JEFFERSON

was appointed a member of the Committee of Correspondence.

Due to illness, Jefferson was not originally a delegate to the First Continental Congress, but in 1775, after his recovery, he was sent to replace his cousin, Peyton Randolph. Soon he was deeply involved in committee work. His paper on "the causes and necessity of taking up arms," attracted the attention of the delegates and established his reputation as a polished and persuasive writer. As a result, he was the overwhelming choice of the Congress to head a committee for drafting a declaration of independence. This committee of five, formed on June 11, 1776, consisted of Thomas Jefferson, chairman, John Adams, Benjamin Franklin, Robert Livingston, and Roger Sherman.

In the meantime, Jefferson had also been writing a proposed constitution for the state of Virginia, but by the time he submitted his draft, the Virginia convention had already adopted one written by George Mason. Nevertheless, the convention voted to use Jefferson's preamble.

The distinguished young Virginian now relinquished the pen to fifty-year-old Benjamin Harrison, the stout, jovial chairman of "the committee of the whole" who had presided over Congress during the vital debates on independence, July 1 and 2. Harrison was a gourmet and looked the part. A prosperous

53

Virginia planter, he owned several large plantations and lived lavishly. Nothing pleased him so much as a good wine, rich food and congenial company. He was an entertaining story teller who laughed infectiously at his own jokes and who was affectionately known as the Falstaff of Congress. For more than 25 years he had held a seat in the Virginia House of Burgesses, having several times been speaker of the house. For all his love of luxury, he had never hesitated to endorse the patriot cause and thereby to risk his life and fortune. Watching him sign the Declaration, William Ellery chuckled as he recalled a remark Harrison had made recently. Turning to slightly built Elbridge Gerry, fat Ben Harrison had said that when it came to hanging the signers, "I shall have all the advantage over you. It will be all over in a minute, but you will be kicking in the air half an hour after I am gone!"

Looked upon as an elder statesman of Virginia, Harrison wielded much influence. He was an intimate friend of George Washington and of Peyton Randolph, who had been president of the Congress until his death in 1775. Of Harrison's many children, seven survived childhood, and one of these, William Henry Harrison, was destined to become the ninth President of the United States. The twenty-third President, Benjamin Harrison, was a great grandson of the signer.

Now Harrison inscribed his name on the great document, his red face serious, but his eyes twinkling with humor. No doubt, thought Ellery, he would offer some wry comment concerning the occasion when he rejoined the other delegates.

Another Virginia delegate noted for his obesity and good humor followed Harrison. He was Thomas Nelson, age thirty-seven, son of a well-to-do merchant of Yorktown, Virginia. He was born December 26, 1738, spent his boyhood in Yorktown, but was sent to Hackney preparatory school in England at the age of fourteen. For eight years he continued his studies abroad, attending Trinity College of Cambridge University, and not returning to Virginia until 1761. As he was then of age, his wealthy father presented him with a plantation and a large house in Yorktown. There Nelson and his wife, the former Lucy Grymes, enjoyed a life of luxury and ease, disturbed only by the natural turmoil created by 11 children. At twenty-six, Nelson had been elected to the Virginia House of Burgesses, where he served until 1774. In that year, the royal Governor Dunmore was presented with a number of resolutions calling upon the British Parliament to redress wrongs done to the colonies. Dunmore promptly dissolved the House of Burgesses, which merely moved in a body to a nearby tavern. There, they formed a provincial legislature and called upon the other colonies to join Virginia in a Continental Congress. Thomas Nelson was elected to the revolutionary legislature and was sent to the Continental Congress in August 1775. Meanwhile he had been commissioned a colonel of a Virginia regiment.

Nelson returned from Philadelphia to attend a session of the Virginia legislature early in 1776, and while there he offered a resolution asking that the Continental Congress declare American independence from Great Britain. When his resolution was passed, he carried it on horseback to Philadelphia, thus setting the stage for Richard Henry Lee's independence resolutions, which in turn led to the formal Declaration of Independence.

Despite his tendency to overweight, Nelson was a vigorous man. His joviality and apparently boundless energy won him a host of friends in the Congress as well as at home in Virginia.

As the next signer came forward, Ellery experienced a sense of disappointment, seeing

that it was Francis Lightfoot Lee, and not the older brother, Richard Henry, author of the original independence resolutions. Richard was still absent from Congress, having rushed to Virginia in June when he learned of his wife's serious illness. Francis, a less colorful political figure than his brother, was nevertheless a staunch patriot. He was born October 14, 1734, at the Lee mansion in Westmoreland County. Brought up with all the easy living of a Virginia country gentleman, he was more prone to seek social pleasures than his serious older brother. The father, Thomas Lee, served for a time as governor of Virginia, and he saw that his sons received a good education from private tutors.

When the elder Lee died in 1750, Francis acquired one of the Lee estates in Loudoun County, Virginia. Eight years later he became a member of the Virginia House of Burgesses, but he was not elected to the Continental Congress until one of the older Virginia delegates resigned in August 1775. A quiet, reticent man, Francis Lee took little part in debates on the floor of Congress, but was a persuasive talker at social gatherings or in small, private groups. As a result, he was an excellent committeeman. He strongly supported his brother's resolutions, voted for independence, and now signed the vital document.

Last of the Virginia delegates to sign on August 2 was Carter Braxton. William Ellery observed that this was the first of the signers who showed no enthusiasm for the task. Braxton's expression was dull, resigned, without emotion, as he lifted the quill pen. Searching his memory, Ellery thought he understood something of the man's feelings, for after the early death of his Virginia-born wife, Judith Robinson, Carter Braxton had gone to England where he made many friends among the leaders of British society. In 1761, he

married again, this time to Elizabeth Corbin, daughter of a British colonel who held the post of Receiver of Customs in Virginia for the King. Braxton's magnificent home became a center of social activity where officials from England as well as leading citizens of Virginia were lavishly entertained.

Braxton was born on his father's tobacco plantation in Newington, Virginia, on September 10, 1736. He received a liberal arts education at William and Mary College, and was still in his teens when he inherited the family estate upon the death of his father. In 1761 he was elected to the Virginia House of Burgesses, where he became intimate with George Washington, Thomas Jefferson, Patrick Henry, and Richard Henry Lee. However, because of upbringing and his family connections he did not share these patriots' zeal for independence from Britain. He did protest mildly against some of the early import taxes, and was prevailed upon to sign a non-importation agreement which had a serious effect on his own business interests. Elected in 1774 to the convention of Virginia patriots, then to the Committee of Safety and the Second Continental Congress, he pursued a conservative course, arguing and voting for conciliation between the colonies and England. He helped to restrain Patrick Henry and some of Henry's angry followers when they threatened to march on Williamsburg to seize a store of gunpowder that Governor Dunmore had impounded. In order to keep the peace, Braxton persuaded his father-in-law, Colonel Corbin, to pay the colonists for the powder and the proposed attack on Williamsburg was abandoned.

Braxton finally went along with the majority, and he now entered his name beneath those of the other Virginia delegates.

Not present for Virginia on August 2 were George Wythe and Richard Henry Lee, both of whom signed at a later date. Wythe was

the lawyer who gave Thomas Jefferson his law instruction. He was born some time in 1726 near Yorktown, Virginia, and like so many of the Virginia signers he grew up in the affluence of a prosperous plantation. He was tutored by his mother in Latin, Greek and mathematics, and this education proved valuable to him when his parents died and his older brother inherited the entire estate. He continued his education at William and Mary College, then studied law as a clerk in the law office of an uncle. About 1750 he began to practice, enjoying considerable success. By the time he was twenty-six, he was a member of the Virginia House of Burgesses. Meanwhile he achieved such a high reputation in his profession that he became generally rated as the foremost lawyer in Virginia.

When the hated Stamp Tax stirred patriot rebellion throughout the colonies, George Wythe wrote the "Resolutions of Remonstrance" which were among the strongest protests to be approved by the Virginia legislature. When the House of Burgesses was dissolved by the governor in 1775 Wythe was elected to the Virginia provincial congress. From there he was sent to the Second Continental Congress where he enthusiastically supported Richard Henry Lee's resolutions on independence. Since he was called back to Virginia to participate in the framing of a state constitution, he took Jefferson's draft with him, but he was absent from Philadelphia during the July debate on independence, and was not on hand for the formal signing on August 2. However, he returned to the Congress later in the month and signed his name to the Declaration August 27, 1776.

Richard Henry Lee, as has been stated earlier, was absent because of his wife's illness, but no man had contributed more to the cause of independence. From the opening session of the Second Continental Congress, Richard Lee was looked upon as a leader, and

as Virginia's most illustrious delegate. As Lee was extremely wealthy, handsome, and influential, much of the early action of the Congress had revolved around him. Although he was a distinguished member of Virginia's landowning class, he favored the abolishment of slavery. He applauded the revolutionary ideas of New Englanders like John and Samuel Adams, and he often expressed a wish to move North, away from the Southern aristocracy.

Born on the Lee plantation in Westmoreland County, January 20, 1732, Richard Henry Lee had known only wealth and graceful living, and had received an excellent education at Wakefield Academy in England. The father, Thomas Lee, was acting governor of Virginia when he died, leaving his property to Richard Henry, who found himself owner and manager of huge plantations at the age of nineteen.

One of Lee's first encounters with British arrogance was in 1755 when, as a captain of the Westmoreland County militia, he offered his troops to General Braddock for a campaign against the French in the French and Indian War. Braddock rejected the Colonials whom he looked upon as untrained and undisciplined provincials. As a result, Lee began to develop an intense dislike for British authority.

In 1757, Richard Henry Lee was elected County Justice of the Peace, and he was sent to the Virginia House of Burgesses a year later. In his first speech to that distinguished body he startled the delegates by advocating abolition of slavery. His association with George Washington and Patrick Henry led him to an early conviction that the colonies had no honorable course but to fight for self government. He helped to establish the Virginia Committee of Correspondence, which he had conceived as early as 1768. There is still some question as to whether he or Samuel

Adams first thought of the idea as a means of unifying the colonies in their quest for independence.

When the House of Burgesses was dissolved, only to carry on their sessions in a nearby tavern, Richard Henry Lee prepared a request to the other colonies, urging that a Continental Congress be established in order "to deliberate on those general measures which the united interests of America . . . require."

Lee organized citizens of his own county to boycott British goods. Called the Westmoreland Association, it was the first group of its kind in America. As a result of his vigorous efforts in behalf of colonial justice, he was sent to the First Continental Congress in 1774. There he served on most of the

RICHARD HENRY LEE

major committees, and as leader of the Virginia delegation and as a polished writer, he was the author of most of the important resolutions adopted by the Congress. One of his more radical resolutions was not passed, however. In it he declared, ". . . as North America is able, willing, and, under Providence, determined to defend, protect and secure itself, the Congress do most earnestly recommend to the several colonies, that a militia be forthwith appointed and well disciplined, and that it be well provided with proper arms."

Later, when he became a delegate to the Second Continental Congress, Lee argued for drastic action with much greater success. Finally, his resolution of June 7, 1776, was adopted:

"Resolved: That these United Colonies are, and of right ought to be, free and independent States, that they are absolved from all allegiance to the British Crown . . . " and so forth.

This document adopted by the Congress was the first official blow to be struck by the United Colonies for independence. In introducing the resolution, Lee spoke with all the eloquence of a deep and abiding conviction.

"Why, then. . .do we longer delay? Why still deliberate? Let this happy day give birth to an American republic. Let her arise, not to devastate and to conquer, but to reestablish the reign of peace and of law."

One can only guess how keen must have been the disappointment of Richard Henry Lee when he could not be present on August 2 for the formal signing of the Declaration. Of greater historical importance was the fact that he would have been the logical choice of Congress to write the Declaration itself, but his enforced absence resulted in the selection of Thomas Jefferson for this important task.

Lee finally returned to Philadelphia and signed the Declaration on September 4, 1776.

NORTH CAROLINA

Salem • Hillsboro • Edenton
• Charlotte
New Bern •
Wilmington •

Wm Hooper

Joseph Hewes,

John Penn

As William Hooper of North Carolina came forward, William Ellery was reminded that this Southern patriot was a Bostonian by birth and had studied law under a veritable firebrand of the Revolution, James Otis. Hooper had moved south to a colony where there had been strong loyalist sentiment, especially since an abortive uprising against a royal governor had failed in 1771. At that time, dissension between "uplanders" and "lowlanders" had led to the arrest of upland leader Harmon Husbands who was imprisoned in Governor Tryon's palace at New Bern. An uplander attack on the palace had been smashed when many North Carolinians rallied to the support of Tryon. Hooper's own father, a Scotch Congregationalist minister, supported the king and was deeply distressed by his son's political activities. Nevertheless, William Hooper steadfastly worked for the colonial cause.

Hooper was born June 7, 1742. Contrary to his father's wishes, who wanted him to enter the ministry, he decided to study law. After graduating from Harvard, he worked in the law office of James Otis who was already engaged in legal battles with the British over the enforcement of various tax measures. Young Hooper absorbed much of Otis' viewpoint in these matters, and he rapidly became an accomplished orator in his own right. After he had passed his bar examination he decided to go south where he was told there were wider opportunities for lawyers. In Wilmington, North Carolina, he met and married Anne Clark, became a success-

ful lawyer, and in 1770 was appointed deputy attorney general for the colony. While he served in this post, the rebellion against the royal governor broke out on North Carolina's western frontier. Hooper urged the use of militia to put down the insurrection, and he fought on the side of the government troops who crushed the frontier forces at the Battle of Alamance, 1771. Two years later, Hooper was elected to the colonial legislature, then to the First Continental Congress in 1774. As a member of the Second Continental Congress he had consistently voted for resolutions condemning British rule, and finally cast his vote for independence on July 4. Although he had initially opposed any form of violent dissent, he saw that compromise with Britain was becoming impossible. In 1775 he wrote, "That our petitions have been treated with disdain, is now become the smallest part of our complaint: ministerial insolence is lost in ministerial barbarity."

Hooper entered his name just to the left of John Hancock's signature, but in a much smaller, neatly executed script.

Next came Joseph Hewes, the second North Carolina delegate who had also been born in a northern colony. Hewes, a prosperous merchant at forty-six, was born in Kingston, New Jersey, January 23, 1730. As a boy he had been interested in ships and trade, had been apprenticed to a merchant in Philadelphia, serving as a countinghouse clerk, and had learned the trade so well that immediately after completing his apprenticeship he set up his own trading firm.

When he was twenty-nine he moved his business to Edenton, North Carolina, an active port on the Albemarle Sound. Soon he acquired a fleet of ships and was admired and respected in his county. In 1766 the community chose him as their representative to the North Carolina legislature. Re-elected time after time, he showed increasing distaste

58

for British rule. He reflected the sentiment of most of his constituents when he spoke vehemently against the Stamp Act, supported various patriot resolutions and became a member of the local Committee of Correspondence. Hewes was a logical choice to serve with North Carolina's delegation to the First Continental Congress. Although he

WILLIAM HOOPER

Royal Governor's residence at New Bern

had been brought up as a Quaker, he did not go along with many Quakers who urged loyalty to King George. Instead, he voted for discontinuance of trade with England if colonial demands were not recognized, despite the serious effect such action would have on his own shipping business. In the Second Continental Congress Hewes served as chairman of the naval committee. When the American navy's first warship was commissioned, Hewes put John Paul Jones in command of the vessel. Having voted for independence on July 4, he now signed the Declaration with a firm hand.

Completing the trio of North Carolina delegates was John Penn, who had only recently moved to Granville County, North Carolina, from Virginia in 1774. Thus none of the three men of this delegation was a native of the state he represented. Penn was born in Caroline County, Virginia, on May 6, 1740, the son of a moderately successful planter. He had received almost no formal education until after his father's death in 1759, when he was

encouraged by an Edmund Pendleton to study law. Pendleton, a justice of the peace, possessed an excellent library, the use of which he offered to young Penn. By the most intensive study, Penn was able to pass his bar examination at the age of twenty-one, but his early years of law practice in Virginia were unrewarding. Finally, in the hope of finding better opportunities, he took his wife, the former Susannah Lynne, and their three children to Williamsboro, North Carolina. There the course of his life suddenly altered for the better. As he interested himself in the patriot movement, he quickly became a leader in his community, was elected to the provincial legislature in 1775 and then to the Second Continental Congress. William Ellery saw Penn as a fresh-faced and pleasant-looking man who appeared to be younger than his thirty-six years. He was quiet, not given to speechmaking and as a result, not too well known to his fellow delegates. But he had voted consistently for independence and now signed the document with enthusiasm.

View of Charleston, South Carolina, engraved about 1739

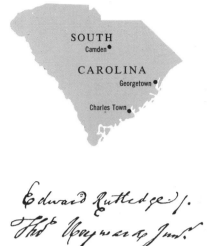

SOUTH
CAROLINA

Camden

Georgetown

Charles Town

Thomas Lynch Junr.

Arthur Middleton

Edward Rutledge J.

Thos Heyward Junr.

The next signer was the youngest of them all — Edward Rutledge, twenty-six, who had only recently returned to America after studying law at the Middle Temple in London. He was born in Charles Town (now Charleston), South Carolina, November 23, 1749, the youngest of seven children. After a period of being privately tutored, he worked in the law office of his older brother, John, who hoped Edward would follow him in the legal profession. When he was nineteen, Edward went to England to complete his study of law, and by the time he came home, in 1773, the colonies were stirring with rebellion. John filled him with genuine fervor for the colonial cause, though both men believed at first that England would be persuaded to see reason in granting the rights Americans demanded.

In 1774, the two brothers, along with Edward's wealthy father-in-law, Henry Middleton, were chosen by the South Carolina legislature to represent the colony in the First Continental Congress. Whatever impression twenty-four-year-old Edward Rutledge may have made on other delegates, he certainly did not impress John Adams favorably. Adams called the young man "a peacock" and "excessively vain, excessively weak. . . and puerile."

Nevertheless, Edward supported the more conservative resolutions and acquitted himself well enough to warrant his being elected to the Second Continental Congress, as was his brother. Not long afterward John was summoned home to prepare the new state constitution and he was elected president of South Carolina.

Without his brother's experienced guidance Edward showed his weakness as he vacillated over the issue of independence. At his request Congress delayed the final vote on the matter from June 7, 1776, the day Richard Henry Lee offered his resolutions, until July 1. When the time for a decision finally arrived, Rutledge and his delegation voted negatively, but on July 2, he reversed himself and voted for the Lee resolutions. Then on July 4, he voted for the Declaration, which he now signed unhesitatingly. Opposition to Britain had only recently been aroused to a high pitch in South Carolina when ten British warships arrived off Charleston on June 4, 1776, and landed troops with the intention of attacking the fort on Sullivan's Island. The offensive was actually launched on June 28, with British infantry under General Clinton attempting to cross the narrow strait from Long Island to Sullivan's, while the fleet pounded the fort with its guns. But the Colonials had returned shot for shot and after a sweltering day of carnage, the British withdrew. They did not return to South Carolina until 1780.

The South Carolinians were a surprisingly youthful group. The oldest member was only thirty-four, and Thomas Heyward, Jr., who now came forward, was thirty. Here was another heir to a prosperous tobacco plantation who had been sent to the Middle Temple in London to study law. Heyward was born July 28, 1746, in St. Helena's Parish, South Carolina, was tutored in Latin and Greek at an early age and apprenticed in a law office for a time before going to England. During his stay in the British Isles he was embittered by the arrogant and contemptuous attitude of Britons toward the "backwoods colonials." By the time he returned to South Carolina, in 1771, he was ready to join the patriots in their efforts to throw off British rule. He became a

EDWARD RUTLEDGE

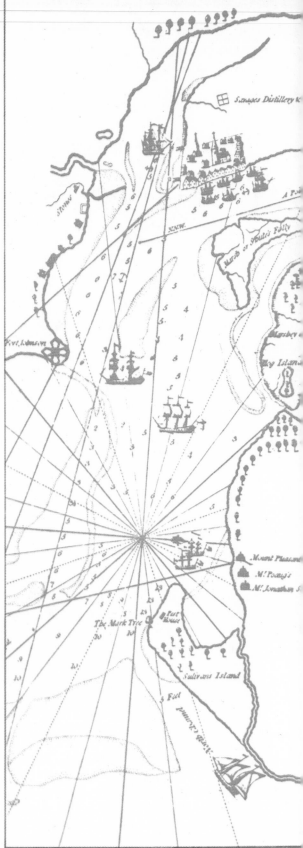

member of the South Carolina Committee of Safety and was appointed with ten other patriots to draw up a state constitution.

When he was twenty-seven, Heyward married Elizabeth Matthews. He had just been elected to the South Carolina assembly, and he served in the provincial Congress after Parliament's passage of the "Intolerable Acts" aroused all of the American colonies to a state of rebellion. Sent to the Second Continental Congress in 1776, young Heyward spoke in favor of the Richard Henry Lee resolutions, voted for them and for the Declaration of Independence.

After Heyward came Thomas Lynch, Jr.,

Left to right
THOMAS HEYWARD, JR.
THOMAS LYNCH, JR.
ARTHUR MIDDLETON

who was Edward Rutledge's senior by less than four months, and was, therefore, the second youngest member of the Congress. He was born on August 5, 1749 in Prince George's Parish, South Carolina, and he grew up on the Lynch plantation while receiving his early education at the Indigo Society School in Georgetown. When he was twelve years old he was sent to school at Eton College in England, and from there to Cambridge University and the Middle Temple in London. However, he took little interest in law, and when he returned home after ten years abroad, he told his father that he had no desire to become a practicing attorney. The senior Lynch generously acceded to his son's wishes and presented him with a large plantation on the Santee River. Young Thomas Lynch then married Elizabeth Shubrick and settled down to become a planter. This was in 1773. But with the exciting political events of the pre-revolutionary period, it was virtually impossible for a young man of Lynch's standing to remain aloof. He was soon commissioned a captain in the South Carolina militia and was appointed to the state constitutional committee.

In the summer of 1775, Thomas Lynch, Jr. was sent on a military recruiting mission that took him into some wild backwoods country. He contracted a fever (possibly malaria) from which he never fully recovered. Shortly after this he learned that his father, who was serving in the Continental Congress in Philadelphia, had suffered a stroke. Young Lynch tried without success to obtain a leave of absence from the militia, but friends used political influence to have him elected as an alternate delegate to the Congress. This automatically released him from military duty and he hastened to Philadelphia, arriving in that city in May 1776. As the father remained critically ill, Thomas Junior took his seat in Congress. He joined in the debate on indepen-

dence, voted for the Declaration, and proudly signed the document in place of his father on August 2. Observing the pallor of this young delegate, William Ellery wondered if he would be able to serve in Congress much longer. As it was to turn out, Thomas Lynch, Jr.'s signing of the Declaration of Independence was the high point of his short life, for from that day he was destined to know only tragedy.

Last and oldest of the South Carolina delegates was Arthur Middleton, thirty-four. He was reputed to be the wealthiest of the delegation, for he owned vast rice and indigo plantations which were worked by hundreds of slaves. He was born June 26, 1742, at the family mansion near Charles Town. His father, Henry Middleton, had been elected president of the First Continental Congress. Like the other three South Carolina delegates, he was educated in England. He attended the Hackney and Westminster preparatory schools, then obtained a bachelor of arts degree at Cambridge. Shortly after his return to South Carolina in 1763 he served as a delegate to the provincial assembly. Young Middleton was handsome, aristocratic and a polished gentleman, yet he plunged heart and soul into the patriot effort to gain colonial rights, raising funds, working on the Committee of Safety, and helping to organize the defenses of "Charles Town," or Charleston. Far more radical in his opposition to the British than was his rather conservative father, he took part in public gatherings and favored a declaration of independence at an early date. In 1776 he became a member of the committee assigned the task of drawing up a state constitution. Then, when his father resigned from Congress in the spring of 1776, Arthur was elected to fill his place. He arrived in Philadelphia in time to vote for independence and to take part in the historic August 2nd signing.

Button Gwinnett

Lyman Hall

Geo Walton.

As the last of the thirteen delegations now approached the table to sign the Declaration, William Ellery experienced a sense of pride and achievement. This was the climax of bitter debate and prolonged tension. Only three men remained to endorse the document that was to rock the world. The first of the Georgia delegates was not well known to Ellery, but he remembered the man's name because of its oddity: Button Gwinnett. In a small, cramped script he penned what was destined to become the rarest of the 56 signatures near the left-hand margin of the parchment.

The exact date of Gwinnett's birth is unknown, but it is generally listed as 1735, in a village called Down Hatherley in Gloucestershire, England. The father was a Welsh clergyman. Evidently the family was not a wealthy one, and Gwinnett received a mediocre education. As a young man he established a small export firm in Bristol, and when he was about twenty-eight he and his wife sailed to America. He settled in Savannah, bought some land on St. Catherine's Island, and established a prosperous plantation. Although he served in the Georgia legislature beginning in 1769, he did little to distinguish himself. But in May 1776, he was elected to the Second Continental Congress. There he argued in favor of independence, voted for the Declaration, and now signed it with a kind of angry determination.

Despite a strong Tory element in Georgia, the members of the Georgia delegation were among the most outspoken supporters of the patriot cause. Such was certainly the case with Lyman Hall, the next signer, who had come originally from New England and who had been largely responsible for getting Georgia represented at the Continental Congress.

Hall was born in Wallingford, Connecticut, on April 12, 1724. With the encouragement of an uncle, he studied theology at Yale University where he graduated in 1747. Soon afterward he married Abigail Burr, and feeling himself unfit for the ministry he decided to take up medicine. By the time he was ready to practice, he decided to move to the south. He went to South Carolina in 1754, but after two years there he settled in Sunbury, Georgia. His medical practice prospered and he bought land to establish a successful rice plantation.

When the Georgia legislature at first refused to send any representatives to the Continental Congress, Lyman Hall summoned an independent citizens' meeting, many of whom were from his own St. John's Parish where patriot sentiment ran high. This convention elected Hall as a delegate to the Second Continental Congress in 1775, but because of the unofficial nature of his selection, he was not at first permitted to vote. However Georgia officially confirmed him as a delegate the following year and sent two other delegates to join him in Philadelphia. The oldest of the signers from Georgia, Hall spoke forcefully for independence and was an enthusiastic signer of the Declaration on August 2nd.

The last of the signers to inscribe the parchment on August 2nd was George Walton, a small, dapper man who appeared younger to William Ellery than he actually was. Walton was thirty-five when he signed the Declaration. He was born in 1741 in Farmville, Virginia, the son of a poor couple who could not afford to send him to school. He was the only Southern delegate who was not a plantation aristocrat. Apprenticed to a car-

Plan of the City SAVANNAH and Fortification.

Profile upon a N.15.E. Line, shewing the Streets, Houses, &c. Wharfs and Fortifications.

penter, he worked for a man who expected him to keep at the job during daylight hours and did not want him to study at night. Since the master carpenter allowed him no candles, young Walton gathered scraps of wood and shavings from the shop and managed to burn them in the privacy of his room where he studied borrowed books. When he was finally released from his apprenticeship he continued to study law books. Then he moved to Savannah, Georgia, obtained a job in the law office of Henry Young, and was eventually admitted to the Georgia bar in 1774. As it turned out, Henry Young was a dedicated loyalist, but Walton became interested in a group of patriots who supported the actions of Boston citizens in their resistance to the British. The Georgia group set up a Committee of Correspondence, and at a meeting in Savannah in early 1775, Walton was appointed secretary of the provincial legislature. He also served as president of the Georgia Committee of Safety.

When Georgia's patriot congress learned of the action of St. John's Parish in sending Lyman Hall to the Second Continental Congress, they decided that they should elect a full delegation to represent them in Philadelphia. But one of these newly appointed delegates was exposed as a loyalist and was recalled. George Walton, elected to replace him, arrived in Philadelphia sometime in March 1776. He voted for independence and he now concluded the signing ceremony with a strong, clear hand, entering his name at the left of the document below the signatures of Button Gwinnett and Lyman Hall.

William Ellery rose from his seat and shook hands with his fellow signers. The job was done; it had not been difficult, nor had it required much time in its accomplishment. But for better or worse, America was now fully and officially committed to go it alone in the face of Britain's military and naval might. It was too sobering a thought for the signers to indulge in a celebration.

PART III

The Aftermath

Such were the men who signed the Declaration of Independence. With few exceptions they were men of property — sober, respected leaders in their communities. Yet the document they had produced and signed broke with centuries of tradition and committed their country to a desperate revolutionary war, the outcome of which appeared dubious even to the most optimistic among them.

Perhaps there were some members of the Congress who still hoped that in the face of such a drastic declaration Britain would recant and enter into negotiations with the newly established United States. Others in their enthusiasm may have believed that aroused Americans would quickly defeat the British troops. It is difficult to imagine exactly what was in the mind of each delegate as he signed his name, but for the most part the signers had no illusions.

For better or worse these courageous rebels had personally endorsed the break from England. Now they must accept the consequences. On that historic day, August 2, 1776, none could predict exactly what these consequences would be. To some the aftermath would bring new opportunities and greater success; to others . . .

Not long after the formal signing of the Declaration of Independence on August 2, 1776, General Howe and a British force of 25,000 men landed on the southwest shore of Long Island, and in a major battle on August 27th the redcoats inflicted nearly twenty percent casualties on the colonial army. General Washington called a staff meeting in Brooklyn Heights at the country estate of signer Philip Livingston, and there it was decided that the American forces should be withdrawn from Long Island. Leaving their campfires burning, the Colonials quietly moved in the night to Harlem Heights. In the morning the British found Washington's camp deserted.

The enraged redcoats proceeded to lay waste much of the countryside. In early September they burned to the ground the fine home of Francis Lewis at Whitestone. Evidently someone had advised the British that Lewis was a leading patriot, for they not only destroyed his property but seized his wife and

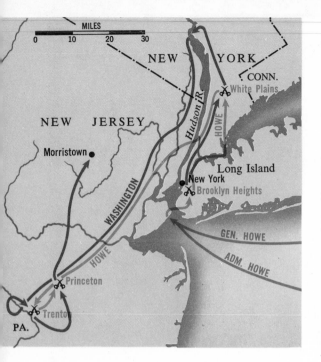

While still serving Congress in Philadelphia, William Floyd learned that his estate in Suffolk County, New York, had been seized. Local Tories aided in ruining what was left of Floyd's farm. They stole his machinery and livestock and removed everything from the house. Meanwhile Mrs. Floyd managed to escape with other members of the family by boat across Long Island Sound to Connecticut. For the entire seven years of the war, William Floyd was unable to return to his home. Nevertheless he served both the Continental Congress and the New York state senate. Later he became a New York representative of the first United States Congress. Floyd died on August 4, 1821, at the age of eighty-six, a highly respected leader of his community.

Another victim of the British campaign in New York was Lewis Morris, whose fine estate in Westchester County, "Morrisania," was sacked and burned while Morris was serving as a militia officer. Morris was one of those signers who clearly foresaw that destruction of his property was likely to follow his endorsement of the Declaration, for the British fleet had been hovering ominously close to New York during the tense debate in Philadelphia. As he had anticipated, British troops despoiled nearly a thousand acres of forest on his estate, ruined the fine house, butchered his cattle and drove his family into seeking shelter with neighbors. At the war's end, he returned to Morrisania and restored it, devoting the rest of his life to managing the estate and serving in the New York senate. He died on January 22, 1798, at seventy-one.

In the autumn, General Howe pushed methodically into Manhattan, and in the end, Washington again was forced to withdraw, this time into New Jersey. Newark fell to British and Hessian troops, and the Colonials retreated toward Trenton.

Members of the New Jersey state legislature followed these reports with great anx-

threw her into a military prison where conditions were intolerable. With no bed and no change of clothes for several months, she suffered cold and privation and her health was permanently impaired. Released two years later in a prisoner exchange, she died shortly after rejoining her family. Lewis was by this time heartbroken and virtually penniless. He nevertheless continued to serve in the Continental Congress until 1779, offering his valuable business experience to committees for the purchase of arms and supplies for the Continental Army. Lewis died on December 31, 1802, at the age of eighty-nine.

Philip Livingston likewise suffered serious losses at the hands of the British forces. His great estate, covering roughly 150,000 acres in Dutchess and Columbia counties, was seized by the occupying army, yet Livingston continued to furnish money to Congress for the conduct of the war. The strain and anxiety he suffered during the first two years of the Revolution had a serious effect on his health. In 1777, after the British had occupied Philadelphia, the Congress fled first to Lancaster, then to York, Pennsylvania. It was there, on June 12, 1778, that Livingston died, less than two years after he had signed the Declaration.

As the British advanced in the fall of 1776, they plundered one farm after another.

iety. Signer John Hart, who had recently left Philadelphia to take his seat in the legislature at Princeton, was personally concerned since his farm lay in the path of the advancing enemy. His fears proved to be well founded. A contingent of Hessian mercenaries who took up quarters in Trenton laid waste Hart's estate, killed his livestock, burned and looted his home and destroyed his valuable grist mills.

Meanwhile, with the British so close, the state legislature fled from Princeton and held meetings when and where the members could assemble in comparative safety. John Hart was sometimes forced to sleep in barns or out-of-doors, as he was never certain of support from local residents, some of whom were loyalists. All this time, he suffered intense anxiety over the situation of his ailing wife and 13 children, since the plundering of his farm had occurred at a time when his wife was gravely ill. By the time Hart was able to return home he found that his wife had died — probably due to lack of care and the hardships imposed by the destruction of their home — and his children were scattered, having taken refuge with various neighbors and friends. As a result of these personal disasters, John Hart's own health began to fail. In 1779, he was forced to retire from the state legislature, and for a brief time he attempted to repair the damage done to his property. But the effort proved too much for him. He died May 11, 1779, at the age of sixty-eight, less than three years after he signed the Declaration and before any end to the war was in sight.

* * *

The British Forces were spreading out and attempting to trap the illusive George Washington. But the wily old fox, as they began to call the American general, was waging the war on his own terms. Washington engaged and withdrew; attacked unexpectedly, only to disappear time and again when the British thought they were about to smash his pitiful army.

But if the British were frustrated, the Americans were close to desperation. Congress was forced to flee time and again, and the members were confronted with one crisis after another. One of the signers, Joseph Hewes of North Carolina, who had at first shown reluctance to approve the Declaration, plunged wholeheartedly into the overwhelming problems of creating a Continental Navy and in helping Washington to plan a campaign. He is said to have worked 12 to 14 hours at a stretch without even taking time to eat. This superhuman effort inevitably took its toll on his health. In the summer of 1779 he began to lose his strength. In the fall he suffered a collapse in Philadelphia and died on November 10, 1779, at the age of forty-nine.

Before the British troops occupied Princeton in 1776 John Witherspoon, president of the College of New Jersey, had closed the college. While the enemy used Nassau Hall as a barracks and destroyed the library with its hundreds of valuable volumes, Witherspoon devoted his time to the Congress. He served on the Board of War as well as on committees involved with foreign relations. Meanwhile his friend and fellow signer, Richard Stockton, had been experiencing serious troubles. Hearing that his family was facing danger in Princeton, he rushed home and managed to take them safely out of the town before the British troops arrived. But as he was attempting to return to Philadelphia, he was betrayed by a loyalist and was captured by enemy soldiers. They threw him into a foul prison because of his part in signing the Declaration of Independence. He was frequently beaten and nearly starved.

Stockton was finally released through the

efforts of Witherspoon and other members of the Congress who arranged an exchange. But by this time Stockton was in poor health. He found that the British had ruined his beautiful mansion, having burned his library and private papers and damaged or removed the furnishings. He remained an invalid until his death at his home, February 28, 1781.

Witherspoon continued as a leading delegate in Congress. He was a strong supporter of confederation of the states, and in 1778 signed the Articles of Confederacy for New Jersey. After the war ended, he spent most of his time working to restore the College of New Jersey. He died November 15, 1794 at the age of seventy-one.

Francis Hopkinson, the lively little man from New Jersey who composed songs and was an accomplished artist, stayed with Congress throughout the war and served as chairman of the Continental Navy Board. He drew up the first sketch of the stars and stripes that was finally adopted as the official United States flag. Hopkinson also designed various government seals, as well as the Great Seal of New Jersey. In late 1776 and again in early 1777, the British ransacked Hopkinson's home in Bordentown. Yet his zeal for the colonial cause never wavered. Besides serving as a popular member of Congress he wrote biting satires criticizing British policies. In 1789, President George Washington appointed him as a federal circuit judge in Pennsylvania. On May 9, 1791, Hopkinson had an attack of apoplexy. He died that day, at the age of fifty-three.

Along with Hopkinson, another New Jersey signer worked in the Congress throughout the war. This was Abraham Clark, as determined a patriot as any of the delegates. As the fighting progressed, his contempt for the British and for American loyalists increased, due in part to the fact that two of his sons fighting for the Continental Army

were captured and cruelly treated by their British captors. In 1777, Clark spoke out angrily against General Washington's offer of amnesty to any former loyalists who would swear allegiance to the United States. Abraham Clark was convinced that the proclamation would permit many traitors to go unpunished. Meanwhile he was keeping a watchful eye on expenditures by the new government. He opposed special bonuses for army officers who, he felt, had sacrificed no more than had many civilians whose only reward was the winning of independence.

Clark served in the New Jersey state legislature between 1784 and 1787 and was sent as a delegate to the Annapolis convention in 1786, when he urged strengthening of the Articles of Confederation. He also represented New Jersey at the Constitutional Convention. With several other signers of the Declaration, he opposed ratification of the Constitution until it should include a Bill of Rights. From 1791 to 1794, he served in the United States House of Representatives, where he favored aiding France in its war with Britain. Abraham Clark died of sunstroke on September 15, 1794, three months after his retirement from Congress. He was sixty-eight.

In the summer of 1777, British General Howe had embarked a large force of 15,000 men on 260 ships and transported them from New York to the northern part of Chesapeake Bay. This massive operation which was a month in its execution was designed to enable the British to take Philadelphia from the south, while General Burgoyne approached the American capital from Albany to the north. Meanwhile, Washington had gathered his army to oppose Howe's advance. At the battle of Brandywine Creek on September 11, the Americans were defeated but, as usual, Washington withdrew with his army still intact, menacing the British occupation of Philadelphia. And although Washington's

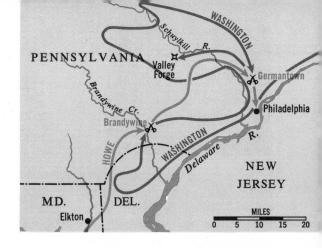

attack at Germantown in October miscarried, it so upset the British that they abandoned further offensive plans for the balance of the year and the ensuing winter while Washington and his men endured the rugged encampment at Valley Forge.

During their advance toward Philadelphia, British troops captured John McKinley, the president of Delaware. As a result, one of the signers of the Declaration, George Read, vice president of Delaware, was called upon to take McKinley's place. After receiving the news in Philadelphia, Read packed up his family and set off for Delaware. On the way he narrowly missed being captured by a British patrol.

After Read arrived home, he took over the administration of the state government, relieving signer Thomas McKean who had assumed the office temporarily. Read served until 1778 when Caesar Rodney was elected. In 1787, George Read was a delegate to the Constitutional Convention and, at his urging, Delaware became the first state to ratify the Constitution. As a member of the Federalist party he was elected U.S. Senator and served in Congress from 1789 to 1793. He then was appointed chief justice of the Delaware supreme court. At age sixty-five, on September 21, 1798, Read died at his home near New Castle, Delaware.

After serving in Congress for a brief period following the signing, Caesar Rodney returned to Delaware. The advancing skin cancer on his face was becoming painful, yet he worked ceaselessly for the war effort. Appointed a major general of the Delaware militia, he led his troops into battle during the bitter winter campaigns of 1776-77. His unit took part in the unsuccessful attempt to defend Philadelphia in 1777. In that year, a loyalist uprising in Sussex County, Delaware, forced Rodney to lead his militia against citizens of his own state, but his decisive action quickly quelled the rebellion which received little popular support. Rodney was elected state president by the Delaware legislature, and despite his serious affliction, he served for four difficult years, during which time the state was menaced by frequent British raids along the coast. By 1782, his health had deteriorated to the point where he was forced to decline reelection as president of Delaware. He was nevertheless appointed a delegate to Congress, although it was understood that he would be unable to serve. Caesar Rodney died on June 29, 1784 in his fifty-fifth year.

Caesar Rodney's friend and associate, Thomas McKean, became acting president of Delaware immediately after John McKinley's capture by the British on September 13, 1777. In a letter to John Adams, McKean described some of his experiences during that period. "I was hunted like a fox by the enemy," he wrote, "and compelled to remove my family five times in a few months." Finally he settled his family in a small log cabin on the Susquehanna River, over a hundred miles from his original residence. McKean signed the Articles of Confederation in 1779, and was chosen the first President of the Congress under the articles on July 10, 1781. McKean also served as chief justice of Pennsylvania, as he had at different times taken residence in both states. Although he did not take part in drafting the Constitution, he was sent to the Pennsylvania ratification convention in 1787. When he was sixty-five he was elected governor of Pennsylvania, serving in this high office from 1799 to 1808, at which time he retired from public service. On June 24, 1817, Thomas McKean died at the age of eighty-three.

Pennsylvania delegates were next in line to suffer losses at the hands of rampaging enemy soldiers. After the British took control of Philadelphia in September 1777, George Clymer's home in Chester County was sacked and Clymer retired from Congress in an effort to take care of his family and to rebuild his fortune. But by December 1777 he was back in Congress. He made a perilous trip to Fort Pitt in severe winter weather to investigate reports of Indian massacres, which he proved were being instigated by the British. In response to Clymer's report, Congress sent a force of 500 men to attack Detroit, but the expedition bogged down for lack of communication and supplies.

Clymer worked closely with financier Robert Morris to set up the first national bank in the United States — The Bank of North America. Morris was having personal troubles of his own. In the course of the war he lost more than a hundred ships, yet he somehow avoided bankruptcy and managed to keep funds flowing into the treasury of the struggling new government. Morris and Clymer remained in Philadelphia when Congress withdrew to Baltimore. Even during the British occupation, they continued their activities in raising money for the war. Robert Morris led a dangerous life during this critical period, often riding alone in the dead of night to meet secretly with European agents at taverns outside of Philadelphia. Many of these agents were persuaded by Morris to furnish large sums of money, arms and other supplies to help the colonial cause.

On one occasion, in 1780, a member of the Congressional War Board by the name of Richard Peters received a letter from Washington stating that the army had nearly exhausted its supply of bullets. At a lavish reception given by the Spanish minister that night, Peters met Robert Morris who noticed that the Congressman looked unusually depressed. Learning of the crisis, Morris disappeared from among the guests, but after a time he reappeared with the news that a privateer had just arrived at his wharf with 90 tons of lead in her hold as ballast. They then arranged to round up 100 volunteers who unloaded the lead while others cast it into cartridges. By morning a great supply of ammunition was on its way to Washington's hard-pressed army.

In 1781, Morris issued over a million dollars of personal credit and raised a loan of $200,000 from France for the final campaign which led to the British capitulation at Yorktown. After the victory, Morris continued to struggle with huge public and personal debts. At one point he wrote a letter of resignation, but Congress persuaded him to stay on. Meanwhile his shipping firm of Willing, Morris and Company, prospered in its trade with China and France. He was elected Senator from Pennsylvania to the first United States Congress in 1788, and he entertained George Washington at the luxurious Morris home at the time of Washington's inauguration as President. Then in 1798 Morris' widely extended finances collapsed and he was sent to debtors' prison in Philadelphia. He was not released until 1801. Embittered and in failing health, Morris lived for a time on an annuity of $1500 a year, but he grew continually weaker and died in comparative obscurity May 8, 1806 at the age of seventy-two.

Morris' wartime associate George Clymer moved to Princeton at the end of the war so that his sons could attend the College of New Jersey. He attended the Constitutional Convention in 1787, was elected to the first United States House of Representatives, and accepted a number of special assignments for President Washington. In his latter years he devoted his time to personal interests, serving as president of the Philadelphia Academy of Fine Arts and the Philadelphia Agricultural Society. He

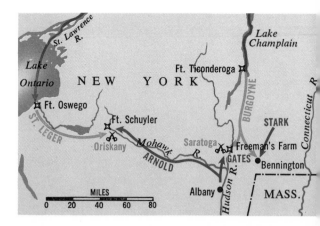

died on January 23, 1813, age seventy-three.

John Morton of Pennsylvania was the first of the signers to die. Morton had rendered an important service in the cause of independence when he cast the deciding vote for Pennsylvania in favor of the Declaration. The opposition to a complete break with England had been strong among the Pennsylvania delegates, and when John Dickinson and Robert Morris were absent, there remained two votes for independence — Franklin and Wilson; and two opposed — Willing and Humphreys. John Morton then broke the tie by voting for independence, although he had been undecided up to that point. As a result of his action many of his friends turned against him. Some of Pennsylvania's conservative Quakers considered him a traitor, and their denunciation of his stand greatly depressed him. In the spring of 1777, he fell ill with a raging fever. Shortly before the end, he told members of his family at his bedside that he was proud of signing the Declaration. "Tell them," he said, "that they shall acknowledge it to have been the most glorious service that I ever rendered to my country." Morton died shortly afterward in April 1777.

During the discouraging winter of 1777-78, the Congress moved to York, Pennsylvania, where its sessions were filled with the gloom of defeat and uncertainty. Then, following the news of the British abandonment of offensive action around Philadelphia, came word of stunning victories in the north. General Burgoyne suffered a major defeat at the hands of General Horatio Gates at Freeman's Farm on the Hudson River, and the British began an agonizing retreat toward Ticonderoga on October 8. But the Americans attacked their rear, then cut off their approach to Ticonderoga, and Burgoyne was forced to surrender on October 17, 1777. These successes bolstered the hopes of the hard-pressed members of Congress, but the dreary winter of 1778 produced little further news to relieve their anxieties.

* * *

One of the vital tasks of the Congress after declaring independence from Britain was the establishment of foreign relations and the enlistment of aid from other governments. At about the time of Washington's encampment at Valley Forge, Benjamin Franklin was in France seeking to persuade King Louis XVI and his war ministers to become an active ally of America. He had been on this mission for many months, having set sail from Philadelphia on October 27, 1776, not long after signing the Declaration. Before leaving, he had given his entire fortune of about 4,000 pounds to the Congress. In Paris, this indefatigable elder statesman proceeded quietly and with his famous good humor to persuade the French that their best interests would be served by sending military aid to the United States.

The surrender of General Burgoyne at Saratoga in October 1777 electrified France, and after months of frustration Franklin began to gain a sympathetic hearing among the French leaders in Paris. He held many talks with the French Minister of Foreign Affairs, Comte de Vergennes who had already been successful in granting arms and money to the beleaguered American Colonies. Finally, Franklin signed a treaty of alliance with France on February 6, 1778. This prompted an offer from the British to negotiate a peace treaty, but as there was no mention of American independence in the offer, Franklin refused to consider it further. Franklin remained in Paris where he helped to implement the French aid and to represent the American government in European councils.

Franklin signed the final treaty of peace with England on September 3, 1783. By this time, he had become universally admired by the people of France and by the diplomats of other nations. There is no doubt that Benjamin Franklin was responsible more than any single individual for winning respect among world powers for the new United States. Not until 1785, when Thomas Jefferson relieved him as American minister to France, did Franklin return to Philadelphia. He arrived in his home city September 14, 1785, to a wild reception — bells rang, bonfires were lighted and artillery salutes were fired.

Yet Franklin's service to his country was not ended. He was elected president of the state of Pennsylvania in 1785 and in 1787, age eighty-one, as a delegate to the Constitutional Convention, he signed the United States Constitution. Three years later, on April 17, 1790, Franklin died in Philadelphia.

A man who played an important role at the Constitutional Convention by assisting the aging Benjamin Franklin was James Wilson of Pennsylvania. After he signed the Declaration, Wilson had withdrawn from Congress and moved to Annapolis during the British occupation of Philadelphia. Until 1782 he devoted most of his time to law practice and to land speculations. Because he had defended some wealthy Philadelphians charged with treason, he became unpopular with the public, and at one time a mob of tradesmen and militia gathered outside his house, opened fire on it with rifles and cannon, while Wilson and his friends fired back. Three people were killed before a troop of cavalry broke up the attack. Later, however, Wilson was elected to Congress and his legal activities were forgotten. As a delegate to the Constitutional Convention in 1787 he became Franklin's spokesman and actually delivered many of

the old gentleman's speeches. Wilson strongly advocated popular vote selection of the President and of members of Congress. He also took part in writing the draft of the Constitution and exerted a major influence on Pennsylvania's ratification of the document. In addressing the state convention, he said, "I am bold to assert that it is the best form of government which has ever been offered to the world." In 1790, James Wilson became an associate justice of the U.S. Supreme Court. He continued to serve in this capacity until his death on August 28, 1798, at the age of fifty-five.

Throughout the bitter winter of 1777, Benjamin Rush, the great Pennsylvania physician, served with Congress while reports of suffering in the field poured in from Washington's headquarters. In April 1777, Rush was appointed physician-general of military hospitals for the Continental Army, and he looked after hundreds of wounded men following the battles of Princeton and Brandywine. Partly because of his desire to improve discipline in the medical department of the army, and partly because of other disagreements with the high command, Rush began to work for the replacement of Washington as Commander-in-Chief. He resigned from his post as physician-general and held no government position until the end of Washington's Presidency. In 1783 he joined the staff of the Pennsylvania Hospital and was instrumental in setting up the first free medical clinic for poor people. When the terrible yellow fever epidemic swept through Philadelphia in 1793, Rush remained and treated hundreds of patients. He contracted the disease, but he recovered and was on hand to attend the sick when a second, equally virulent epidemic struck in 1798. Always politically active he attended the Pennsylvania convention to ratify the U.S. Constitution, and in 1797 he was given the position of Treasurer of the United States

Mint in Philadelphia. Rush was sixty-seven when he died, April 19, 1813.

* * *

As the war ground on, William Paca, signer from Maryland, continued to serve in Congress, and was a member of Maryland's state senate from 1777 to 1779. He was also appointed chief judge of Maryland's superior court in 1778. All this time he was pouring thousands of dollars of his personal fortune into outfitting and arming American regiments. He worked on the committee that drafted Maryland's state constitution, and at the war's end he became governor of Maryland, from 1782 to 1785. In 1789, President Washington appointed him as a United States district judge. Paca died in 1799 at the age of fifty-eight.

While Paca worked so vigorously to establish a new state government for Maryland, Charles Carroll, the only Roman Catholic signer, was also serving on the Maryland legislature and on the state constitutional drafting committee. Carroll made certain that full religious freedom became an integral part of the Maryland constitution. He was re-elected as a state senator for over 25 years, and he was also elected to the first United States Senate that convened in 1789, resigning from this position in 1792 to keep his Maryland senate seat. Carroll retired from public service in 1804, but he enjoyed an active life for many more years. In 1828 he took part in marking the foundation of the Baltimore and Ohio Railroad. He was the last surviving signer of the Declaration when he died at the age of ninety-five on November 14, 1832.

Samuel Chase of Maryland was one of the most active members of Congress during the first two years following the signing of the Declaration. He is credited with serving on at least 30 committees, among them one having the responsibility of restricting Tory ac-

tivity. But in 1778, Chase was accused of dishonest business practice when it was claimed that he had used information received in Congress to make a personal profit from selling flour to the army. As a result Chase was recalled from Congress. He went back to his law practice and gradually regained the confidence of the people in Maryland. In 1791 he was appointed chief justice of Maryland's general court, and five years later, George Washington chose him as an associate justice of the Supreme Court. Despite a fine legal mind, Chase became involved in political attacks on Jeffersonians being tried under the notorious Sedition Acts. His bias led to impeachment proceedings in 1804. He was acquitted and remained on the bench for the rest of his life. He was seventy when he died of gout on June 19, 1811.

A less colorful member of the Maryland delegation was Thomas Stone, whose quiet modesty kept him in the background of Congressional debate. He nevertheless worked diligently on committees, including the one assigned to drafting the Articles of Confederation. In 1777 he was elected to the Maryland state senate where he served for the rest of his life. He attended the Congress of Confederation at Annapolis in 1783 and was selected to represent Maryland at the Constitutional Convention of 1787. However, he declined this honor as his wife was seriously ill. When Mrs. Stone died that summer at the age of thirty-four, Stone retired from public life. He became deeply melancholy and died on October 5, 1787. He was only forty-four at the time of his death.

While many of the signers of the Declaration were suffering privation and hardships brought on by the war and by British vengeance, a number of them continued to serve in Congress, suffering more anxiety than actual hardship. Both Josiah Bartlett and William Whipple of New Hampshire remained in Philadelphia during the balance of 1776, and Whipple remained with Congress during the anxious months of 1777-1778. Bartlett helped to draft the Articles of Confederation for a proposed union of states, then in 1779 he served his home state as chief justice of the court of common pleas. Later he became chief justice of the New Hampshire superior court. When the states were voting to ratify the United States Constitution in 1788, Bartlett was a leader in persuading the people of New Hampshire to go along. When the first National Congress assembled, Josiah Bartlett was appointed by the state legislature to attend as a senator, but he refused the appointment because of his age and waning health. He did, however, accept the presidency of New Hampshire in 1790, serving one term. Within a year afterward, in 1795, he died at the age of sixty-five.

Bartlett's fellow signer, William Whipple, remained active in Congress until 1779. As he had been appointed a brigadier general of militia in New Hampshire, he spent some of this time in his home state recruiting and training troops, and he led a New Hampshire brigade in the Battle of Saratoga in October 1777. It is said that on this expedition he took a Negro slave with him, and prior to the engagement, Whipple told his man that he was expected to fight bravely for his country. The slave shook his head, saying that he had no reason to fight, but would be inclined to defend his liberty, if he had it, to the last drop of his blood. Whipple gave the slave his freedom on the spot.

Upon Burgoyne's surrender, Whipple was assigned by General Gates to the task of escorting the prisoners of war to a Boston campsite. He later took part in an unsuccessful campaign to drive the British from Rhode Island. In 1780 Whipple was elected to the New Hampshire legislature, and two years later he became associate justice of the state superior court. He died in 1785 of a heart ailment.

Meanwhile another New Hampshire delegate, Matthew Thornton, had also served the Congress for about a year after the signing, then returned to New Hampshire to become an associate justice of the superior court. He retained this office until 1782, when he retired at the age of sixty-eight. For the remaining years of his life he lived on his farm near Merrimack, New Hampshire, and he died June 24, 1803, age eighty-nine.

Proud and vain as he was, no member of the Independence Congress was more open-handed or more courageous than John Hancock. After he resigned as President of the Congress in 1777 he retained a seat as a delegate from Massachusetts, but for a time he took more interest in military matters. In 1778 he took command of the Massachusetts militia. Commissioned a major general, he led some 6,500 men in a campaign designed to drive the British from Rhode Island. The plan called for naval support from a powerful French fleet that had arrived in American waters to aid the Colonials on July 8, 1778. The French Navy was to bombard the British at Newport, Rhode Island, then land a body of French troops while Americans under General John Sullivan, along with John Hancock's New Englanders, attacked from the land side. Hancock led his men out of Providence in mid-July, and the battle began to unfold. But dissension between Sullivan and the French command slowed the campaign, and by August a full scale offensive had not been launched. Before the French troops could be put ashore, a violent storm scattered the fleet, and the French sailed north to Boston for repairs. The Americans engaged a strong British force, but were forced to withdraw.

John Hancock's brief military career ended in 1779 when he took part in the Massa-

76

Unfinished portrait
of American peace commissioners
in Paris

chusetts constitutional convention and, upon adoption of the state constitution, was elected the first governor in 1780. For five years he served as the Massachusetts chief executive, living and dressing as lavishly as any previous royal governor. His magnificent coach was pulled by six horses, and his liveried servants accompanied him wherever he went. Elected again in 1787, he continued as governor for the rest of his life. Selected to head the Massachusetts convention to ratify the United States Constitution, Hancock played an important role, persuading his delegates to vote for ratification. By this action he won great popularity and hoped to be put forward as the first President of the United States, but as with his ambition to take supreme command of the army, this hope was dashed — again by George Washington. Hancock died, still in the office of governor of Massachusetts, on October 8, 1793.

It is a curious fact of the signers' story that one of the most colorful delegates, Samuel Adams, led a comparatively quiet life after the signing. For a few months, during late 1776 and the gloomy year of 1777, Adams continued to be one of the resolute Congressmen who helped to keep the shaky government from falling apart. He encouraged wavering delegates to have faith in their cause. "Better tidings will soon arrive," he insisted. "Our cause is just and righteous, and we shall never be abandoned by Heaven while we show ourselves worthy of its aid and protection." In 1779, Sam Adams helped John Adams compose a state constitution for Massachusetts, but he soon retired from Congress. He served the Massachusetts state senate for a time, and he opposed ratification of the United States Constitution until a bill of rights was added to it. As time went on, he seemed to lose his old revolutionary zeal, and although he was elected lieutenant governor of Massachusetts under Governor John Han-

cock, he accomplished little of importance during that period. In 1794, after Hancock's death, he was elected governor, an office he held for three more years. At the age of seventy-six, in 1798, Adams retired. He spent his remaining years weighed down by illness and poverty, and he died October 2, 1803.

By contrast, Samuel's cousin, John Adams, remained in the national limelight and was destined to become the second President of the United States. In the early years of the Revolution he served on numerous Congressional committees and is credited with being chairman of at least twenty-five of them. As chairman of the Board of War, he occupied one of the key positions in the new government. Then he followed Benjamin Franklin to Paris in February 1778, to assist in the vital negotiations for French aid.

On his return to America, John Adams was elected to the Massachusetts state constitutional convention, where he played a major role in drafting a document that became a model for many other states. When Franklin notified Congress in 1779 that Britain was making overtures toward peace, Adams was appointed minister plenipotentiary to negotiate a treaty of peace with Great Britain. He set sail in October 1779, but did not arrive in Paris until February 1780. By that time England was no longer desirous of making peace. Unable to accomplish his original mission, Adams was assigned a new task — to negotiate a loan from the Netherlands. For two years he struggled to win the confidence of the Dutch, finally succeeding in gaining from them recognition of the United States. The Netherlands signed treaties of trade in 1782 and authorized a loan of eight million guilders.

77

Governor Elbridge Gerry's role
in redistricting Essex County, Massachusetts,
into a dragon-like shape
gave rise to a new political word —
"gerrymander."

This move, coupled with the French assistance that Franklin had arranged, and the British military reverses in America, finally brought Britain to the conference table, and John Adams joined Henry Laurens, John Jay and Benjamin Franklin in Paris for the peace talks. A temporary treaty was signed November 30, 1782, but a final agreement was not reached until September 3, 1783.

Adams remained in Europe as a foreign minister to the Netherlands and England until 1788. Immediately after his return to America he became involved in the selection of a chief executive in the new federal government. Many of his friends were endeavoring to elect him President, but as Washington was clearly the popular choice, John Adams was proposed for Vice President. He won this position in 1789, but looked upon it with considerable disdain. "My country," he said, "has in its wisdom contrived for me the most insignificant office that ever the invention of man contrived."

After Washington's retirement, a genuine political campaign developed between the Federalists, supporting John Adams, and the Anti-Federalists who backed Thomas Jefferson. Under the regulations of that time, Adams was elected President with 71 electoral votes, while Jefferson, with 68 votes, automatically became Vice President.

Adams' presidency was not a particularly happy one. He became increasingly unpopular with the public for his determined stand to avoid involvement in a war between England and France. There was strong pressure for supporting France, and this became an issue in the election of 1800. Adams lost the election by only a handful of votes, and bitterly resented Jefferson's selection which, because of a tie vote between Jefferson and Aaron Burr, was decided in the House of Representatives.

John Adams retired to his home in Quincy, where he led a quiet life for 25 years. He lived to see his oldest son, John Quincy Adams, elected President in 1825. The following year, on July 4, 1826, Adams lay near death. "Thomas Jefferson still survives," he whispered. But Jefferson also died on the same day — the fiftieth anniversary of the adoption of the Declaration of Independence.

Signer Elbridge Gerry of Massachusetts was especially interested in military affairs, and he served on several Congressional committees involved in furnishing arms and supplies to the army. In 1785 he returned to Massachusetts where he was elected to the state legislature. Representing his state at the Constitutional Convention, he objected to many of the Constitution's provisions, and in the end refused to ratify it. As time went on he took a cynical view of democracy which, he felt, was "the worst of all political evils." Nevertheless he was elected to the U.S. House of Representatives in 1789, and spent much of his term arguing for amendments to the Constitution. He was sent by President John Adams as one of three commissioners to France in 1797. The other two men, Charles Pinckney and John Marshall soon left France in a disagreement over demands by French officials seeking bribes, but Gerry remained and for doing so, was severely criticized in America.

After his return home, Gerry was elected governor of Massachusetts in 1810 and served until 1812. He was then nominated to run for Vice President of the United States with James Madison, and was inaugurated March 4, 1813. He never completed his term, for on his way to the Capitol on November 23, 1814, the seventy-year-old Vice President became ill and died in his carriage.

Soon after signing the Declaration, Oliver Wolcott of Connecticut took an active part in the army. As a brigadier general, then major general of militia, he was in the thick of fighting in New York and Connecticut. He

commanded several thousand volunteers and marched to Saratoga where he joined the forces of General Gates. In October 1777, he participated in the capture of British General Burgoyne and his army. For a brief period in 1778, Wolcott served again in Congress while it was meeting in York, Pennsylvania, but the following summer he was once more in command of a Connecticut division, charged with defense of the state's seacoast. During this difficult period the British invasion of Connecticut laid waste the towns of Fairfield and Norwalk. Families fled to the woods for safety while enemy soldiers looted and burned their homes. Wolcott's army fought the invaders constantly through 1779, and was ultimately successful in driving the British out. Following the war, in 1786, Wolcott became lieutenant governor, then governor of Connecticut ten years later. After a little over a year in office, he died on December 1, 1797, age seventy-one.

* * *

Meanwhile a number of other signers devoted their energies to serving in Congress or in other branches of government. Robert Treat Paine served Congress until late 1777 when he became attorney general of Massachusetts. He was appointed a justice in the Massachusetts supreme court and retired in 1804 at the age of seventy-three. He died May 11, 1814. After the signing, Stephen Hopkins remained in Congress a brief time, did not attend any sessions in 1777, but returned as a delegate in 1778. He retired to his home in Providence in 1779, and died there in 1785 at the age of seventy-eight.

William Ellery, the man who had watched the faces of the signers so intently on August 2, 1776, had remained in Congress and served on a number of committees. While thus engaged, he was informed of the British invasion of his home state of Rhode Island and learned that his home in Newport had been burned. After the British withdrew from Newport, late in 1779, Ellery returned home to look after his family and property. He repaired his home and attended to his law practice and business interests in Rhode Island, then returned to Congress where he served from 1781 to 1785. Ellery's legal knowledge was invaluable to some of the committees on which he served. He was chosen to study the peace treaty with Britain, and he supported a resolution in 1785 to abolish slavery in the United States. After President Washington gave him the post of collector of customs for Newport, he served in that capacity for 30 years. On February 15, 1820, when Ellery was ninety-two years old, his physician stopped in to see him. Feeling no pulse, he insisted that the old gentleman take a glass of wine. "I have a charming pulse," said Ellery, "but why concern yourself. I am going off the stage of life and it is a blessing that I go free from sickness, pain or sorrow." Later that day he went quietly to his room where, propped up in bed, he read a copy of Cicero. In the evening his daughter found that he had died. He appeared to have fallen asleep over his book.

Roger Sherman of Connecticut devoted his time during the war to serving in Congress and on the superior court of his home state. He was on the committee to draft the Articles of Confederation, signed the Articles in 1778, and worked hard to see that they were ratified by all the states. At sixty-six, in 1787, he was selected as a representative of Connecticut to the Constitutional Convention, which met in Philadelphia. When serious arguments arose at the convention over the inequalities of representation between large and small states, Sherman made a number of proposals that satisfied the delegates and became known as the "Connecticut Compromise." By this compromise all states were given equal representation in the Senate. He signed the Constitution on September 17, 1787, and gave his wholehearted support to it in essays he wrote for Connecticut journals. When he was sent to the House of Representatives in 1789, Sherman helped to prepare the Bill of Rights and fought for its inclusion as an amendment to the Constitution. His final service to the country was as United States Senator. He died at age seventy-two, while still in office, on July 23, 1793.

In his efforts to keep the struggling Revolutionary Government from collapsing, William Williams sacrificed most of his personal wealth. He signed promissory notes to help finance the offensive against Ticonderoga, and in 1779 he converted large amounts of gold and silver to Continental paper money that became virtually worthless. During the campaigns of 1780 and 1781, he invited French officers to occupy his house in Lebanon, Connecticut. After helping to establish the Articles of Confederation, and later the Constitution, he served on the Connecticut governor's council for nearly 20 years. He died in 1811, at the age of eighty.

Samuel Huntington, of Connecticut, was a member of Congress for ten years following the Declaration of Independence. In 1778 he signed the Articles of Confederation, and when John Jay resigned as president of the Congress in 1779, Huntington was elected to fill his place. He was still the leader of Congress when the Articles of Confederation were ratified by Maryland, the last of the states to do so, in 1781. Shortly afterward, due to poor health, Huntington resigned and returned to Connecticut. There he served as an associate justice of the superior court. He then returned to Congress in 1783 while the legislature was meeting in Princeton, New Jersey. He was lieutenant governor of Connecticut in 1785 and governor one year later, winning reelection each year thereafter for ten consecutive years. Huntington was sixty-

four when he died on January 5, 1796.

Like Huntington, James Smith of Pennsylvania served Congress for a time, then resigned to become a judge of the Pennsylvania court of appeals. Reelected to Congress in 1785, he refused the position because of his advancing years. He continued in law practice for a few more years but was no longer active in politics. He died July 11, 1806, at eighty-seven.

Less than a year after signing the Declaration, George Taylor of Pennsylvania returned to his home in Easton because of ill health. For a time he served on the Pennsylvania executive council, but he soon was forced to give this up, too. He died on February 23, 1781, at the age of sixty-five.

Although signer George Ross of Pennsylvania took little part in Congress after 1776, he devoted himself to work on relations with the Indians, and helped to consummate a treaty with the tribes in northwestern Pennsylvania. Ross was the uncle of Betsy Ross' husband, John Ross. Legend has it that he accompanied George Washington and Robert Morris to the widow Ross' upholstery shop on Arch Street in Philadelphia where the first stars and stripes banner was being made. George Ross suffered a severe case of gout, attributed to his love of rich foods. He was only forty-nine when he died in Philadelphia on July 14, 1779.

* * *

Some of the Virginians who had played important roles in the independence movement were less prominent in the affairs of the new United States. George Wythe, for example, became involved in Virginia affairs after signing the Declaration. He became a judge in 1778, then accepted a position as professor of law at William and Mary College. This was the first such chair of law in an American college. In 1790 he founded his

own law school. There were suspicious circumstances surrounding his death at age eighty in 1806, as a Negro cook in the household testified that Wythe's grandnephew and heir to the estate had poisoned the old man. However, under Virginia law at that time, a Negro's testimony was not admissable and the case was dropped.

Richard Henry Lee, whose famous resolutions provided the first real step toward independence, lost popularity with Virginia voters when rumors were falsely spread that he was really a Tory, loyal to England. An official inquiry by the Virginia legislature cleared him of the charges, but for a time he seemed to lose prestige. During his term in Congress, he signed the Articles of Confederation. In 1778, while commanding a unit of Westmoreland County militia, he and his men engaged British forces that were plundering the Virginia countryside. After a brief period of army service, he was elected to the state legislature. In 1784 he became president of Virginia, but remained in that office for only a year. He was elected to the United States Senate in 1789, served for three years, then retired due to failing health. Lee was sixty-two when he died at his estate in Westmoreland County on June 19, 1794.

The stout, jovial man who had presided over the debates on independence as chairman of the committee of the whole, Benjamin Harrison, returned to Virginia in the fall of 1777. There he served in the Virginia legislature for a time, then became governor of Virginia in 1782. He was a firm administrator during the difficult period of the state's formation as an independent commonwealth, and was reelected for another term. He retired to private life at the end of his second term, though almost immediately afterward he was sent to the House of Burgesses. Again, in 1791, he was elected governor, but following a lavish party on the day

after his election, he fell seriously ill and died that night, April 24, 1791.

Francis Lightfoot Lee of Virginia retired from Congress in 1779. Although he spent several years in politics, serving on the Virginia legislature, his later life was comparatively uneventful. He lived quietly on his plantation in Richmond County, and died there at the age of sixty-two on January 11, 1797.

Only nine days after signing the Declaration, Carter Braxton returned to Virginia where he took his former seat in the state legislature, representing King William County. He continued to hold this position for many years and chaired a number of important committees, including the committee of the whole. As the war progressed, virtually every one of the merchant ships in which he had an interest was sunk or captured by the British. As a result he was forced to sell his land holdings and he fell more and more deeply into debt. Still, his neighbors continued to send him as their representative to the state legislature. On October 10, 1797 in his sixty-first year, he died of a stroke.

* * *

Farther south, in Georgia, a signer with military ambitions had ended his career in tragedy. Given the governorship and a military command in 1777, Button Gwinnett found himself at odds with General Lachlan McIntosh, who objected to Gwinnett's assuming supreme command of the Georgia troops. As governor, Gwinnett felt he had the right to direct the army and he ordered an ill-fated expedition against British positions in Florida. When McIntosh publicly denounced this poorly executed campaign, Gwinnett challenged the general to a duel. Early in the morning of May 16, 1777, the two men, with their seconds, met in a pasture, and with great formality took their stands several paces apart. They fired pistols almost simultaneously. Both men were hit, and although they were apparently not seriously hurt, Gwinnett died of his wounds on May 27. He was forty-two years old.

* * *

Late in 1778 and early in 1779, the war began to shift toward the south. British warships began to appear off the coasts of Georgia and South Carolina, while transports from New York, loaded with troops, landed a large fighting force at the mouth of the Savannah River. Another British unit was ordered north from Florida, threatening to squeeze Savannah in the jaws of a pincer movement.

To meet this threat the Americans had a force of about 1,000 men under North Carolina's General Robert Howe. This pitiful army was quickly overwhelmed as the British seized Sunbury, Savannah and Augusta. Soon the entire state of Georgia was in enemy hands.

This occurred while Lyman Hall was still serving Congress in Philadelphia. He learned some time later that his rice plantation had been leveled by the British in 1778, but fortunately his family managed to escape to the north. Eventually he was able to bring them to Philadelphia. In 1782 Hall returned to Georgia where he was elected governor. He held the office for only a year and retired to a newly established plantation in 1784. He died on October 19, 1790, age sixty-six.

In 1778 signer George Walton was appointed colonel of a Georgia regiment by the state legislature. American General Robert Howe was charged with defending Savannah when British forces under Colonel Campbell were landed for an attack on the city. With only 800 men in his command, Howe hoped to block the enemy's entrance into Savannah, and he might have succeeded had not an American defector shown Campbell a safe route across a swamp for an attack on the defenders from the rear. During the ensuing battle, George Walton was wounded in the thigh and captured. Shortly afterward he was released in a prisoner exchange. Walton was almost immediately appointed to the governorship of Georgia, and less than a year later, in January 1780, he was returned to Congress. He next served a full term as governor, then became chief justice for the state of Georgia. In 1798 he was elected to the United States Senate. He retired a year later and died on February 2, 1804, at the age of sixty-four.

In the spring of 1780, British General Sir Henry Clinton landed a strong contingent of troops on the coast near Charleston, South Carolina. While British warships lay offshore to blockade Charleston, Clinton led his army inland, crossed the Ashley River and surrounded the city. By May, cut off by land and sea, the American General Benjamin Lincoln was forced to surrender.

During the attack on Charleston, signer Edward Rutledge was captured by the British. Rutledge had left Congress early in 1777, to lead contingents of South Carolina militia and to shore up the defenses of his state. In command of a corps of artillery during the siege of 1780, he attempted to bring his troops to the aid of General Lincoln and was seized in the course of the resulting battle. He was held in Charleston as a prisoner of war, but after General Lincoln's unconditional surrender, British General Cornwallis grew nervous about the possibility of a secret uprising of the citizens. One night squads of soldiers were sent through the city to round up civil and military officers, many of whom were

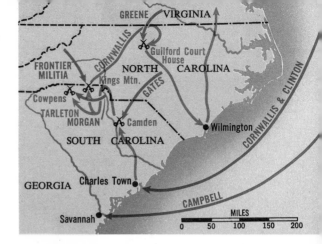

roused from their beds and herded into the Exchange near the waterfront. Rutledge was among the assembled prisoners. His mother was taken from their country home and placed under house arrest in the city. Next day Rutledge, along with a large number of other prominent citizens, was put on a British guard ship that soon set sail for St. Augustine, Florida. He was held in a military prison for over a year before being released in a prisoner exchange. He then returned to a practice of law in Charleston. For several years, until 1798, he was a member of the state legislature. Then he was elected governor of South Carolina. He was only fifty when he died before the end of his term, on January 23, 1800.

Thomas Heyward, Jr. had left Congress in 1778 to become a circuit judge in his native South Carolina. At the time he took office his responsibilities exposed him to considerable danger, for the British were consolidating their positions near Charleston, and some Tories in the vicinity threatened to betray him. Nevertheless, Heyward showed no hesitation in trying a number of men accused of aiding the enemy. While the British advanced to within a few miles of Heyward's court, he calmly sentenced the convicted traitors to hanging and saw that the executions were carried out. As the British moved on Charleston in 1779 he donned his uniform as an artillery captain and led his unit into heavy fighting around Port Royal Island. He was with Edward Rutledge in a skirmish with the British at Beaufort in 1780, and in that action was seriously wounded. Then, shortly after the capture of Charleston, he was taken prisoner by enemy troops and sent with Rutledge to the St. Augustine prison. While he was confined there for several months British soldiers raided his plantation, burned the buildings and carried off his slaves. His wife became ill and died before he was released. In 1781

he returned to Charleston where, despite his losses, he vigorously resumed his work as a circuit judge and continued in this office until 1789. He died at age sixty-two on his plantation in 1809.

Another South Carolina signer to be captured and imprisoned by the British was Arthur Middleton, who returned from Congress early in 1778 to participate in the defense of his state. Although he had been elected the first governor of South Carolina under its newly adopted state constitution, he declined acceptance of the position as he doubted the legality of some of the assembly's actions. During the British invasion, Middleton's large estate was ravaged along with most of the plantations in the area, but he made no attempt to protect it, realizing that his first duty was to the state militia. He instructed his wife to take the family out of the area and joined with Rutledge in the defense of Charleston. When the city fell to the British, he was taken prisoner and sent to St. Augustine. Released in a prisoner exchange a year later, he returned to Congress in Philadelphia, where he served until 1782. Then at the war's end he devoted his energies to rebuilding his estate. While serving in the state legislature, he contracted a fever in 1787, and died on January 1, 1788, at the age of forty-four.

The only South Carolina delegate not involved in the defense of Charleston was Thomas Lynch, Jr. This unfortunate young man, who had signed the Declaration for his father when the latter became ill, had left Philadelphia in the fall of 1776. The father and son were both in poor health as they journeyed slowly to the south, and Thomas

83

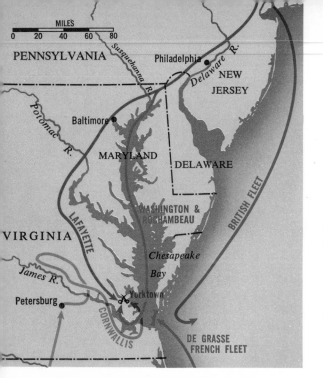

Left
The final campaign, 1781
Right
Nelson home
after the siege of Yorktown

MILES
0 20 40 60 80

PENNSYLVANIA

Susquehanna R.

Philadelphia

Delaware R.

NEW JERSEY

Potomac R.

Baltimore

MARYLAND

DELAWARE

VIRGINIA

LAFAYETTE

James R.

Petersburg

WASHINGTON & ROCHAMBEAU

Chesapeake Bay

Yorktown

CORNWALLIS

BRITISH FLEET

DE GRASSE FRENCH FLEET

British occupation than they would be as hunted fugitives. For himself, he chose the latter course and fled before the raiders arrived. With their usual vindictiveness, the British troops burned the estate and left Hooper's home in ruins. Hooper continued as a member of the North Carolina legislature till the end of the war, then resumed law practice. He died at the age of forty-eight on October 4, 1790.

About the time of Hooper's flight from the British, John Penn of North Carolina returned home from Congress. He was immediately given a powerful position on the North Carolina board of war, charged with the responsibility of supplying the militia. Partly due to his successful efforts, Francis Marion and his guerrillas were kept supplied, and the American troops succeeded in forcing the army of Lord Cornwallis into retreat before the end of 1780. John Penn remained in Stovall, Granville County, North Carolina, practicing law. Like Hooper, he died at an early age, forty-seven, in September 1788.

* * *

In 1780, the war in the South began to move to its conclusion, and although the American cause in many respects appeared hopeless, some signs appeared that foretold the ultimate British collapse. The daring lightning cavalry attacks of Francis Marion's guerrillas were beginning to take a serious toll of the Cornwallis forces as they moved north through North Carolina. General Nathanael Greene's army was steadily gathering strength while the British Army was being eroded. Early in 1781, Greene moved against the British encampment in Hillsboro, North Carolina, with a force of some 4,000 men. In March 1781 there was a violent battle at Guilford Court House, from which the Americans withdrew only after inflicting heavy casualties on Cornwallis' army.

---

senior died before they reached home. For two years young Lynch fought unsuccessfully to regain his health, but finally on the advice of his doctor, he and his wife set sail for the south of France. But the ship disappeared at sea with all on board. It was never heard from again. This was in 1779, and at age thirty, Lynch was the youngest of the signers to die.

With nearly all of Georgia, and with Charleston, the jugular of South Carolina, under British control, General Clinton confidently wrote a dispatch to London in June 1780, indicating that war in the South was nearing a successful conclusion for the Crown. He then turned his command over to Lord Cornwallis and returned by ship to New York. To the Americans, the situation was perhaps the bleakest of the war.

As the war moved into North Carolina, signer William Hooper was engaged in law practice in Wilmington and was serving on the state legislature, having left Congress in 1777. The British advance in 1780 brought them to Wilmington, close to Hooper's plantation. Somehow the British were advised that a notorious patriot lived not far away, for they dispatched a band of raiders to capture Hooper. Warned of the approaching enemy party, Hooper sent his family into Wilmington where he felt they would be safer under the

Greene began a series of attacks on British supply lines in South Carolina, while Cornwallis' main army struggled northward toward Virginia. Action slowed as the raging heat of summer burned the swamps and plains of the Carolinas.

Meanwhile the great state of Virginia, virtually immune from military action until late in the war, was experiencing the terror and destruction of an invasion. British-Tory troops under Benedict Arnold had landed near Westover in January 1781, and were soon overrunning the eastern countryside. When Arnold encamped along the James River for the winter, Washington decided to send a well-trained force of about 1500 men to Virginia with support of elements from the French Navy. While the Americans marched south, Cornwallis moved up into Virginia to augment Arnold's smaller army. By the time the Americans under Lafayette had reached Richmond, they numbered about 3,000, while the augmented British Army had swelled to nearly 7,500. Then began a series of engagements in which the Continentals fought their usual harassing actions, always withdrawing before a full-scale battle could destroy them.

One of the Virginia signers became deeply involved in the climactic period of the war. This was Thomas Nelson, Jr. who had returned to Virginia from Congress due to an illness in 1777. Before the end of that year, Governor Patrick Henry commissioned Nelson a brigadier general in command of Virginia militia. The appointment came at a time when a British invasion of Virginia appeared imminent. But then the enemy warships turned north and the threat was ended.

When the British finally did invade Virginia in 1781, Thomas Jefferson was ending his term as governor. Jefferson recommended that Nelson, a military man, take his place. While Nelson struggled to defend the state with inadequate forces at his command, he was forced to call hundreds of young men from their farms. Realizing the hardships being imposed on their families, General Nelson assigned many of his own field hands to help smaller farms with their harvests. He also distributed huge sums of money to more than a hundred families. Then in August 1781, he was advised by General Washington that the French fleet, acting in unison with General Greene's army from the south and Lafayette's forces from the north, would attempt to trap Cornwallis at Yorktown.

Nelson himself led some 3,000 Virginia militia against the British, and on September 18, 1781 he met with Washington, Lafayette and their aides on board the French flagship of Comte de Grasse to plan the siege of Yorktown. During the siege that followed, the house of Nelson's uncle was commandeered by the British to serve as Cornwallis' headquarters. While some 16,000 American troops closed in, the guns of the French fleet bombarded the town, and the elder Nelson's fine home was leveled. Meanwhile, Thomas Nelson, Jr. was observing the action of his own artillery. Noticing that the gunners were shelling all parts of the town except the vicinity of his mansion, he asked the crews why they avoided that particular section.

"Out of respect to you, sir," was the reply.

Nelson stepped up to one of the cannon, aimed it directly at his house and lit the fuse.

An old account of this incident is a masterpiece of understatement: "Governor Nelson

85

... at once directed fire upon his house. At that moment a number of British officers occupied it, and were at dinner enjoying a feast, and making merry with wine. The shots of the Americans entered the house, and killing two of the officers, effectively ended the conviviality of the party."

After three weeks of siege, Cornwallis asked for a parley. His historic surrender came on October 19, 1781.

Thomas Nelson, Jr. remained in the office of governor for only a month after the siege of Yorktown was lifted. His health had been steadily deteriorating and he retired permanently from public life. Although he was elected a delegate to the Constitutional Convention, he declined. He died on January 4, 1789, at his quiet country home in Hanover County.

* * *

The author of the Declaration of Independence, Thomas Jefferson, did not remain long in Congress after he had signed the document. Instead he decided to serve his own state and accepted a seat in the Virginia Assembly to which he had been elected. In the fall of 1776, when Franklin was appointed to negotiate a treaty with France, Jefferson declined an offer to accompany the elder statesman and continued to work with the state legislature. He assisted George Wythe and Edmund Pendleton in revising Virginia laws. In the course of this assignment he proposed the first laws in the South forbidding the importation of slaves, establishing public schools, and guaranteeing broad rights in religious freedom.

As Governor Patrick Henry's term ended in June 1779, Jefferson was elected to take his place. Then, within a few months, Virginia was invaded by Benedict Arnold's troops, and the army of Cornwallis moved up from the south. A large section of Richmond was destroyed; fires raged all along the James River, and when the marauding army approached Jefferson's home, he narrowly escaped capture. He was greatly relieved, in 1781, to turn the governorship over to General Thomas Nelson, Jr., fellow signer of the Declaration.

Jefferson then retired to his estate, but again he was threatened with capture, this time by the notorious Colonel Tarleton. Jefferson had been warned that a British raiding party was in the vicinity and had sent his family away in a carriage. He had then returned to his room to gather up some papers when he saw a troop of enemy cavalry coming up a hill toward the house. He seized a sheaf of papers from his desk, rushed to a side door and leaped into the saddle of his horse just as the cavalry came clattering up the carriageway at the front of the house. Jefferson spurred his horse across a meadow and into the woods without a second to spare.

The war had barely ended when Jefferson was overcome with grief at the death of his wife in 1782. To keep his mind occupied, he sought a return to public service and was appointed minister plenipotentiary to assist in negotiating a final treaty with Great Britain. But before he could leave for England, an acceptable treaty draft was submitted to Congress and his trip was canceled. He then served in Congress for two years, during which time he conceived of the decimal money system and the dollar unit for the United States. In May 1784, he sailed to France, accompanied by his eldest daughter, Martha, to join Franklin and John Adams in

The White House, executive mansion for two presidents who were signers of the Declaration, John Adams and Thomas Jefferson

a mission for establishing trade relations with various European countries. Jefferson then took Franklin's place as minister at the French court, and served in this capacity until 1789. He next became Secretary of State in George Washington's first cabinet. As time went on, Jefferson found himself differing more and more with Washington's policies and more particularly with those of Secretary of the Treasury, Alexander Hamilton. Finally he resigned in 1793.

In the Presidential election of 1796, Jefferson opposed John Adams. He received the second largest number of popular votes and became Vice President in accordance with the law at that time. Again, in 1800, Jefferson sought the Presidency. This time he succeeded after a tie electoral vote was settled in the House of Representatives. In his inaugural address, Jefferson commended the nation to "a wise and frugal government, which shall restrain men from injuring one another, which shall leave them otherwise free to regulate their own pursuits of industry and improvement, and shall not take from the mouth of labor the bread it has earned."

He was reelected in 1804 by an overwhelming vote. During his eight-year administration he negotiated the Louisiana purchase and authorized the Lewis and Clark expedition to explore the continent west of the Mississippi. His management of foreign relations was exceptionally skillful at a time when the fledgling nation was attempting to gain respect.

Although Jefferson and John Adams had become political enemies, after Jefferson's retirement to Monticello the two signers reestablished their former friendship and engaged in voluminous correspondence. In 1818 Jefferson founded the University of Virginia. He acted as its rector for the remainder of his life.

The end came in 1826, when Jefferson was eighty-three years old. He became very ill in June of that year, and on the third of July he asked those at his bedside what day of the month it was. On being told, he expressed a wish that he might live until the Fourth, which would mark the fiftieth anniversary of the country's independence. The next morning he handed his daughter a leather case in which he had placed his epitaph:

Here was buried
THOMAS JEFFERSON
Author of the Declaration of Independence,
Of the Statute of Virginia for
Religious Freedom,
And Father of the University of Virginia

By noon of the Fourth of July 1826, Thomas Jefferson had died. He was not aware that by an uncanny coincidence his friend John Adams died on the same day.

The story of America's quest for independence had come full circle, but the great Declaration that had flowed from Jefferson's pen 50 years earlier belonged to every generation. It will continue to inspire new generations as long as mankind struggles to free itself of tyrannical government.

"I have sworn upon the altar of God, eternal hostility against every form of tyranny over the mind of man."
— THOMAS JEFFERSON

How the Document Was Preserved

The ink was scarcely dry on the parchment after fifty-one of the fifty-six signers had put their names to it on August 2, 1776, before the question arose as to its safekeeping. At first it was placed in the custody of the Secretary of Congress, Charles Thomson, who had attested Hancock's signature on Jefferson's original draft. When Philadelphia was threatened by invasion, Congress adjourned on December 12, 1776, and moved to Baltimore. The Declaration was transported there, along with other government papers, in a horsedrawn wagon. After about two months in Baltimore, the document was taken back to Philadelphia. Then, in September 1777, the British advance forced Congress to move again. They took the Declaration to Lancaster, then to York, Pennsylvania, where it remained for a little over a year.

In 1779, Congress and the parchment were back in Philadelphia, but only four years later, in 1783, it was taken to Annapolis, then to Princeton in the same year. In 1784 it was in Trenton, and a year later when the seat of government was shifted to New York City, it was moved again. The document was stored in the old New York City Hall on Wall Street, a structure that was later remodeled into the Federal Building.

When Thomas Jefferson was appointed Secretary of State in 1790, he kept the Declaration in his temporary offices on lower Broadway. Shortly afterward, the document was taken back to Philadelphia where it was kept somewhere on Market Street, then in a building at Fifth and Chestnut Streets.

Not until 1800 was the Declaration moved to Washington, D.C. It was stored in the Treasury Building at 19th and Pennsylvania Avenue for a few months before it was transferred to the War Office Building on 17th Street. There it remained until 1814, when, during the War of 1812, a British force approached the capital. Within sound of rifle and cannon fire, Secretary of State James Monroe ordered the parchment removed for safekeeping. It was placed in a linen bag and transported by wagon to a barn on the farm of Edgar Patterson. After a night in the barn it was taken to Reverend Littlejohn's home in Leesburg, Virginia, where it was safely stored for a few weeks. When the British troops were withdrawn from Washington, it was brought back to the 17th Street War Office Building.

In 1823, Secretary of State John Quincy Adams requested that a facsimile of the Declaration be made by a transfer process, but in the course of making the transfer, a considerable amount of the original ink was removed. Meanwhile, since curious visitors were permitted to examine the parchment, the constant rolling and unrolling began to damage the surface seriously. Still, no one seemed to be greatly concerned. Secretary of State Daniel Webster decided to put the Declaration on public view in a glass-enclosed frame. It was placed on display on the second floor of the Patent Office at 7th and F Streets. Unfortunately, the frame hung opposite a window that allowed full sunlight to fall on the parchment for prolonged periods causing the aging ink to fade. After thirty-five years in this location, the Declaration was sent to the Philadelphia Centennial Exposition of 1876.

By this time the precious document was warped and cracked, the script was growing faint, and some of the signatures were all but indistinguishable. At a ceremony during the Centennial, Richard Henry Lee, grandson of the signer, read the document to a large crowd. Then the Declaration was placed in a glass-enclosed case to be viewed by thousands of visitors to the Exposition.

At the close of the fair, the parchment was taken back to the Patent Office in Washington. Concerned about deterioration of the paper and ink, Congress ordered a study to be made of methods of restoration and preservation, but none of the "experts" consulted was able to offer a practicable solution.

Shortly after the Declaration was moved to a new State Department Building in 1877, the Patent Office burned to the ground. A further effort at restoration of the parchment was made in 1880 when a committee asked William R. Rogers, president of the National Academy of Sciences, to conduct new studies. All that these studies produced was a recommendation to keep the Declaration in a dark place. Thirteen years later, in 1893, the document was put in a steel case and stored in the State Department basement. No one could see it without special permission of the Secretary of State.

A 1903 committee came up with the suggestion that the Declaration and the Constitution be placed between thick panes of glass and put on view at the Library of Congress, but no action was taken.

During the Harding administration in 1921, Librarian of Congress Herbert Putnam drove to the State Department in a Model T Ford mail truck, took the two documents to his own office and had them mounted between double sheets of glass, with a layer of special gelatin designed to screen out actinic rays. These invaluable "sandwiches" were then mounted in a marble and bronze display case.

During the Second World War, on December 23, 1941, the documents were carefully removed from the case, covered by acid-free manila paper, inserted into a container made of all-rag neutral millboard which was then sealed with tape. Next the millboard was put into a bronze container and this was heated to 90° F for several hours in order to remove moisture. Finally the container was sealed with lead, surrounded by rock wool, deposited in a heavy box and secretly transported to Union Station. There it was carried into a Pullman compartment for a journey to Fort Knox. During its wartime stay there, experts repaired the Declaration by painstakingly filling microscopic holes and cracks in the parchment.

Returned to the Library of Congress on September 19, 1944, the documents were again put on display, protected by an armed guard twenty-four hours a day.

When the present National Archives Building was constructed, the plan included a special hall for valuable papers. Then on December 13, 1952, accompanied by an armed escort, the Declaration and the Constitution were taken in an armored truck to the new building. There they may be seen today, fully protected from light damage and magnificently encased for public view.

The Declaration on display
at the National Archives

The Declaration of Independence

IN CONGRESS, JULY 4, 1776.

When, in the course of human events, it becomes necessary for one people to dissolve the political bands which have connected them with another, and to assume, among the powers of the earth, the separate and equal station to which the laws of nature and of nature's God entitle them, a decent respect to the opinions of mankind requires that they should declare the causes which impel them to the separation.

We hold these truths to be self-evident: — that all men are created equal; that they are endowed by their Creator with certain unalienable rights; that among these are life, liberty, and the pursuit of happiness. That, to secure these rights, governments are instituted among men, deriving their just powers from the consent of the governed; that whenever any form of government becomes destructive of these ends, it is the right of the people to alter or to abolish it, and to institute new government, laying its foundation on such principles, and organising its powers in such form, as to them shall seem most likely to effect their safety and happiness. Prudence, indeed, will dictate that governments long established should not be changed for light and transient causes; and, accordingly, all experience hath shown that mankind are more disposed to suffer, while evils are sufferable, than to right themselves by abolishing the forms to which they are accustomed. But, when a long train of abuses and usurpations, pursuing invariably the same object, evinces a design to reduce them under absolute despotism, it is their right, it is their duty, to throw off such government, and to provide new guards for their future security. Such has been the patient sufferance of these colonies; and such is now the necessity which constrains them to alter their former systems of government. The history of the present King of Great Britain is a history of repeated injuries and usurpations, all having, in direct object, the establishment of an absolute tyranny over these states. To prove this, let facts be submitted to a candid world.

He has refused his assent to laws the most wholesome and necessary for the public good.

He has forbidden his Governors to pass laws of immediate and pressing importance, unless suspended in their operation till his assent should be obtained; and, when so suspended, he has utterly neglected to attend to them.

He has refused to pass other laws for the accommodation of large districts of people, unless those people would relinquish the right of representation in the legislature — a right inestimable to them, and formidable to tyrants only.

He has called together legislative bodies at places unusual, uncomfortable, and distant from the depository of their public records, for the sole purpose of fatiguing them into compliance with his measures.

He has dissolved representative houses repeatedly, for opposing, with manly firmness, his invasions on the rights of the people.

He has refused, for a long time after such dissolutions, to cause others to be elected; whereby the legislative powers, incapable of annihilation, have returned to the people at large for their exercise; the State remaining, in the meantime, exposed to all dangers of invasion from without, and convulsions within.

He has endeavored to prevent the population of these states; for that purpose obstructing the laws for the naturalization of foreigners; refusing to pass others to encourage their migration hither, and raising the conditions of new appropriations of lands.

He has obstructed the administration of justice, by refusing his assent to laws for establishing judiciary powers.

He has made judges dependent on his will alone for the tenure of their offices, and the amount and payment of their salaries.

He has erected a multitude of new offices, and sent hither swarms of officers to harass our people and eat out their substance.

He has kept among us, in times of peace, standing armies, without the consent of our legislatures.

He has affected to render the military independent of, and superior to, the civil power.

He has combined with others to subject us to a jurisdiction foreign to our constitutions, and unacknowledged by our laws; giving his assent to their acts of pretended legislation:

For quartering large bodies of armed troops among us;

For protecting them, by a mock trial, from punishment for any murders which they should commit on the inhabitants of these states;

For cutting off our trade with all parts of the world;

For imposing taxes on us without our consent;

For depriving us, in many cases, of the benefits of trial by jury;

For transporting us beyond the seas, to be tried for pretended offences;

For abolishing the free system of English laws in a neighboring province, establishing therein an arbitrary government, and enlarging its boundaries, so as to render it at once an example and fit instrument for introducing the same absolute rule into these colonies;

For taking away our charters, abolishing our most valuable laws, and altering, fundamentally, the forms of our governments;

For suspending our own legislatures, and declaring themselves invested with power to legislate for us in all cases whatsoever.

He has abdicated government here, by declaring

us out of his protection, and waging war against us.

He has plundered our seas, ravaged our coasts, burnt our towns, and destroyed the lives of our people.

He is at this time transporting large armies of foreign mercenaries to complete the works of death, desolation, and tyranny, already begun with circumstances of cruelty and perfidy scarcely paralleled in the most barbarous ages, and totally unworthy the head of a civilized nation.

He has constrained our fellow-citizens, taken captive on the high seas, to bear arms against their country, to become the executioners of their friends and brethren, or to fall themselves by their hands.

He has excited domestic insurrections amongst us, and has endeavored to bring on the inhabitants of our frontiers the merciless Indian savages, whose known rule of warfare is an undistinguished destruction of all ages, sexes, and conditions.

In every stage of these oppressions we have petitioned for redress in the most humble terms; our repeated petitions have been answered only by repeated injury. A prince whose character is thus marked by every act which may define a tyrant is unfit to be the ruler of a free people.

Nor have we been wanting in attentions to our British brethren. We have warned them from time to time, of attempts by their legislature to extend an unwarrantable jurisdiction over us. We have reminded them of the circumstances of our emigration and settlement here. We have appealed to their native justice and magnanimity; and we have conjured them, by the ties of our common kindred, to disavow these usurpations, which would inevitably interrupt our connections and correspondence. They, too, have been deaf to the voice of justice and of consanguinity. We must, therefore, acquiesce in the necessity which denounces our separation; and hold them, as we hold the rest of mankind, enemies in war, in peace, friends.

We, therefore, the representatives of the United States of America, in General Congress assembled, appealing to the Supreme Judge of the world for the rectitude of our intentions, do, in the name and by the authority of the good people of these colonies, solemnly publish and declare, that these united colonies are, and of right ought to be, free and independent states; that they are absolved from all allegiance to the British Crown, and that all political connection between them and the state of Great Britain is, and ought to be, totally dissolved; and that, as free and independent states, they have full power to levy war, conclude peace, contract alliances, establish commerce, and to do all other acts and things which independent states may of right do. And, for the support of this Declaration, with a firm reliance on the protection of Divine Providence, we mutually pledge to each other our lives, our fortunes, and our sacred honor.

The foregoing Declaration was, by order of Congress, engrossed and signed by the following members: —

JOHN HANCOCK

NEW HAMPSHIRE
JOSIAH BARTLETT
WILLIAM WHIPPLE
MATTHEW THORNTON

MASSACHUSETTS
SAMUEL ADAMS
JOHN ADAMS
ROBERT TREAT PAINE
ELBRIDGE GERRY

RHODE ISLAND
STEPHEN HOPKINS
WILLIAM ELLERY

CONNECTICUT
ROGER SHERMAN
SAMUEL HUNTINGTON
WILLIAM WILLIAMS
OLIVER WOLCOTT

NEW YORK
WILLIAM FLOYD
PHILIP LIVINGSTON
FRANCIS LEWIS
LEWIS MORRIS

NEW JERSEY
RICHARD STOCKTON
JOHN WITHERSPOON
FRANCIS HOPKINSON
JOHN HART
ABRAHAM CLARK

PENNSYLVANIA
ROBERT MORRIS
BENJAMIN RUSH
BENJAMIN FRANKLIN
JOHN MORTON
GEORGE CLYMER
JAMES SMITH

GEORGE TAYLOR
JAMES WILSON
GEORGE ROSS

DELAWARE
CAESAR RODNEY
GEORGE READ
THOMAS McKEAN

MARYLAND
SAMUEL CHASE
WILLIAM PACA
THOMAS STONE
CHARLES CARROLL
 OF CARROLLTON

VIRGINIA
GEORGE WYTHE
RICHARD HENRY LEE
THOMAS JEFFERSON

BENJAMIN HARRISON
THOMAS NELSON, JR.
FRANCIS LIGHTFOOT LEE
CARTER BRAXTON

NORTH CAROLINA
WILLIAM HOOPER
JOSEPH HEWES
JOHN PENN

SOUTH CAROLINA
EDWARD RUTLEDGE
THOMAS HEYWARD, JR.
THOMAS LYNCH, JR.
ARTHUR MIDDLETON

GEORGIA
BUTTON GWINNETT
LYMAN HALL
GEORGE WALTON

Bibliography

Augur, Helen, *The Secret War of Independence*. Duell, Sloan & Pearce, New York, 1955.

Becker, Carl, *The Declaration of Independence: A Study in the History of Political Ideas*. Alfred A. Knopf, New York, 1960.

Becker, Carl, *The Declaration of Independence*. Peter Smith, New York, 1933.

Bowen, Catherine Drinker, *Miracle at Philadelphia*. Little, Brown and Company, Boston, 1966.

Boyd, Julian, *The Declaration of Independence: The Evolution of the Text*. Princeton University Press, Princeton, 1943.

Boyd, Julian P., ed., *The Papers of Thomas Jefferson*. Princeton University Press, Princeton, 1950.

Brotherhead, William, *The Book of the Signers*. W. Brotherhead, Philadelphia, 1861.

Burnett, Edmund C., ed., *Letters of Members of the Continental Congress,* 8 vols. Carnegie Institute of Washington, Washington, D.C., 1921-36.

Chidsey, Donald Barr, *The Dramatic Story of the First Four Days of July 1776*. Crown Publishers, Inc., New York, 1958.

Chinard, Gilbert, *Honest John Adams*. Little, Brown and Company, Boston, 1933.

Editors of AMERICAN HERITAGE, *The American Heritage Book of the Revolution*. American Heritage Publishing Co., Inc., New York, 1958.

Ford, Worthington Chauncey, *Journals of the Continental Congress 1774-1789*. Government Printing Office, Washington, D.C., 1904.

Goodrich, Charles, *Lives of the Signers of the Declaration of Independence*. Reed & Company, New York, 1829.

Hawke, David, *A Transaction of Free Men: The Birth and Course of the Declaration of Independence*. Charles Scribner's Sons, New York, 1964.

Irving, Washington, *Life of George Washington*. G. P. Putnam & Co., New York, 1857-59.

Lossing, B. J., *Biographical Sketches of the Signers of the Declaration of Independence*. Davis, Porter & Co., Philadelphia, 1866.

Malone, Dumas, *The Story of the Declaration of Independence*. Oxford University Press, New York, 1954.

McGee, Dorothy Horton, *Famous Signers of the Declaration*. Dodd, Mead & Company, 1955.

Ross, George E., *Know Your Declaration of Independence and the 56 Signers*. Rand, McNally & Company, Chicago, 1963.

Sanderson, John, and Waln, Robert, Jr., *Biography of the Signers to the Declaration of Independence,* 9 vols., R. W. Pomeroy, Philadelphia, 1820-27.

Sinclair, Merle, and McArthur, Annabel Douglas, *They Signed for Us*. Duell, Sloan and Pearce, New York, 1957.

Thompson, Charles O. F., *A History of the Declaration of Independence*. Published by the Author, Bristol, R.I., 1947.

Tourtellot, Arthur Brown, AMERICAN HERITAGE — *We Mutually Pledge to Each Other, Our Lives, Our Fortunes and Our Sacred Honor*. American Heritage Publishing Co., Inc., New York, December 1962, Vol. XIV, Number 1.

Whitney, David C., *Founders of Freedom in America*. J. G. Ferguson Publishing Company, Chicago, 1964.

Index

Credits

The Granger Collection: pages 9, 29, 67, 81, 86. Independence National Historic Park Collection: page 19. Library of Congress: pages 15, 17, 21, 22, 40–41, 65, 79. Metropolitan Museum of Art, Edward W. C. Arnold Collection, photograph courtesy Museum of the City of New York: page 35. New York Public Library — Map Division: pages 24, 62 — Prints Division, I. N. Phelps Stokes Collection: pages 12, 35, 53, 60 — Rare Book Division: page 39. North Carolina State News Office, Dept. of Conservation and Development: page 59. Rhode Island Historical Society: page 31. Smithsonian Institution: page 16. United Press International: page 85. Henry Francis du Pont Winterthur Museum: pages 27, 77.